PUFFIN BOOKS

PROFESSOR BRANESTAWM'S PERILOUS PUDDING
and Other Incredible Adventures

In this new collection of stories, Professor Branestawm's well-intentioned but erratic inventions cause chaos once again in Pagwell. The Professor sets his mind to creating a dress-zipping machine, a self-washing car, a mobile church, a press-button shop and a perfect pudding. However, nothing seems to work out in quite the way he intends. It's just as well that the inhabitants of Pagwell are used to the pandemonium caused by the Professor's loony inventions!

Readers of about eight to ten are most likely to enjoy the Professor's escapades. There are many more books about him published in Puffin, including one for younger readers: *Professor Branestawm's Pocket Motor Car*.

Norman Hunter

PROFESSOR BRANESTAWM'S PERILOUS PUDDING
and Other Incredible Adventures

Illustrated by Derek Cousins

PUFFIN BOOKS

Puffin Books, Penguin Books Ltd, Harmondsworth, Middlesex, England
Penguin Books, 625 Madison Avenue, New York, New York 10022, U.S.A.
Penguin Books Australia Ltd, Ringwood, Victoria, Australia
Penguin Books Canada Ltd, 2801 John Street, Markham, Ontario, Canada L3R 1B4
Penguin Books (N.Z.) Ltd, 182–190 Wairau Road, Auckland 10, New Zealand

First published by The Bodley Head 1979
Published in Puffin Books 1983

Printed and bound in Great Britain by
Cox & Wyman Ltd, Reading
Set in Baskerville

To my three beautiful granddaughters,
Deirdre, Gillian and Jennifer,
with love

CONTENTS

1 Professor Branestawm's Perilous Pudding, 9
2 Automobile Ablutions, 19
3 Mrs Flittersnoop's Invention, 31
4 Press-Button Shopping, 42
5 The Vicarage Tree, 52
6 The Professor's Um-ah-brella, 64
7 Rainbow Roads, 74
8 A Date with Miss Frenzie, 85
9 The Big Zipper, 93
10 The Great Cake Scandal, 103
11 The Invention that Was too Successful, 115
12 The Branestawm Church Service, 125

I

Professor Branestawm's Perilous Pudding

Mrs Flittersnoop was worried about the pudding.

'I really don't know what to do, I'm sure,' she said. 'I do want it to be something special, but I can't make up my mind.'

The Professor was giving a highly special lunch party, to which a number of exceedingly vippy people were coming: Lord and Lady Pagwell, and the Mayor and Mayoress of Great Pagwell, as well as several other rare and valuable people. No wonder Mrs Flittersnoop wanted to do something special.

She'd hunted through all her recipe books. And she had enough to sink two cookery schools. She looked through recipes she'd cut from magazines and hadn't had time to stick into scrap-books. But she still couldn't make up her mind what sort of special pudding to make.

The Professor offered to invent a special VIP pudding for her. But she said, 'No, indeed, I'm sure, sir, thank you very much.' For Mrs Flittersnoop had had some of the Professor's cooking inventions before and was reasonably scared of them.

But the Professor wasn't very good at taking 'No' for an answer where his inventions were concerned. And he felt it was his duty to help Mrs Flittersnoop, whether she liked it or not. 'One must, um, ah, sometimes do things for people for their own, um, ah, good,' he said to himself, because he remembered his old schoolmaster used to say that to him when he made him do things he'd much rather not have done.

So while Mrs Flittersnoop continued her search for an ecstatic pudding recipe, the Professor set to work to prepare a little something he could secretly add to Mrs Flittersnoop's pudding to make it more successful.

'I know what I'll do, sir,' she said to the Professor one glittering morning. 'I've found a recipe for lemon and strawberry sponge soufflé surprise. As long as I can make it rise nicely it should be a great success. I always was a light hand with pastry, so perhaps I can manage this. One never knows what one can do till one tries, I always say.'

That gave the Professor a clue for his invention. He went secretly into his inventory and eventually produced a very innocent-looking powder that was guaranteed to help any pudding rise to any occasion.

It took a bit of doing to get the powder secretly sprinkled into Mrs Flittersnoop's pudding mixture, because she was popping about the kitchen a bit much on the morning of the lunch party. But the Professor went round to the front door and rang the bell. Then while Mrs Flittersnoop went to see who it was, the Professor quickly mixed his pudding-rising powder into the pudding before she came back.

All was ready for the great Pagwell-shaking lunch party. Mrs Flittersnoop had laid the table with the best cloth and the special-best cutlery, china and glass. She'd got out and polished some extremely untouchable silver, all to make the important guests think the Professor always lived like that. But it didn't, because the important guests always got out all their fancy bits and pieces when they had guests, hoping their guests would think that they always lived like that. But the guests didn't think it because they did the same themselves. People are a bit funny.

The lunch was being an enormous success. Lord Pagwell told all his favourite jokes and remembered how they ended, for a change. Lady Pagwell had some nice fruity high-class gossip, which went down almost as well as the food. The Mayor, in spite of getting his chain of office a bit damp in the soup, enjoyed himself immensely because he didn't have to make a speech after

FLOU

the lunch, which he often did after lunches and he found it gave him butterflies in the tum and that spoilt his appetite. The Lady Mayoress said nothing and said it very nicely. Colonel Dedshott and Commander Hardaport (Retired) told each other about their military and naval experiences, but neither of them believed them. And Mrs Flittersnoop, obstructed willingly by her sister Aggie, served everything up beautifully and didn't take anyone's plate away until they'd finished.

Then in came the famous pudding.

Mrs Flittersnoop had thought of putting a fanfare of trumpets on the record player to give the pudding a good entrance, but they hadn't got a record of trumpet fanfares. Colonel Dedshott would have brought some of his Catapult Cavalier trumpeters if he'd known about the special pudding, and Commander Hardaport would have been delighted to get sailors to pipe the pudding aboard.

But it was greeted with such *oohs!* and *ohs!* of delight that any other music was unnecessary.

'I do hope you'll like it, Your Lord and Ladyship, madams and sirs,' said Mrs Flittersnoop as she served it.

Lord Pagwell ate as much as he could manage and found to his surprise that he had rather more left on his plate than he had to start with.

The Mayor demolished his pudding, but it caught up with him and he still had a plateful to go.

Lady Pagwell nibbled in well-bred fashion, but the pudding on her plate got bigger instead of smaller.

Oh dear! Was that secret ingredient of the Professor's going to start things?

Colonel Dedshott fought a losing battle with his pudding, which began bubbling and rising all over the table-cloth. Commander Hardaport (Retired) was pushed off his chair and capsized as his pudding took command.

Then the pudding in the dish Mrs Flittersnoop was holding began rising and bubbling and overflowing.

'Oh my goodness me, indeed, I'm sure, sir!' she cried. She hurriedly took the offending pudding out into the kitchen, but it pushed her against the wall and went swelling and rolling out into the hall.

Inside the dining-room the guests had to scramble out of the windows, which they found easier than they expected as the swelling pudding helped them on their way.

Oh, disaster! Oh, catastrophe! The frightful pudding went on growing. Nothing could stop it. It rolled out of the house and across the road like a lemon- and strawberry-flavoured volcanic eruption, only worse.

'I can't understand it, I'm sure, sir,' gasped Mrs Flittersnoop as she fought her way over the ramping pudding. 'The recipe never said anything about doing this.' Then she caught the Professor's eye. And she thought he looked a bit sort of thingummy. Of course, it might have been due to having to stamp over the pudding, but then again. . . .

'You didn't, sir, if I might make so bold,' she said, 'happen to put anything in the pudding, sir, did you? I mean to say I hardly like to mention it, but . . .'

'Well, um, ah, yes, Mrs Flittersnoop,' said the Professor, shaking lumps of fierce pudding off his boots, 'I must, um, ah, tell the truth. It would be most unscientific not to.' He could also see from the look on Mrs Flittersnoop's face that it wouldn't be any use not to.

'I, er, as a matter of fact I did add just a touch of um, ah, something to make sure the pudding would rise. You were so anxious about it I, um, ah, did not wish you to be disappointed.'

'Oh dear, oh dearie me!' cried Mrs Flittersnoop, waving her arms, partly in despair and partly to ward off a rather affectionate helping of pudding that was putting its arm round her waist.

'That recipe already had things in it to make the pudding rise. You really shouldn't have done it, sir, I'm sure.'

The Professor couldn't answer, he was being swept down the garden path by a tidal wave of lemon and strawberry pudding.

Things were awful. Lord and Lady Pagwell's car was stuck in a morass of pudding. The Mayor and Mayoress were running down the road with hot pudding in hot pursuit.

'I'd never have agreed to be Mayor if I'd known it meant being chased by pudding!' the Mayor cried.

Colonel Dedshott, waist deep in pudding, was on the phone calling out the Army. Commander Hardaport (Retired) had retired up a tree, which was the nearest thing to a ship's mast he could find. He was used to dealing with rough seas, but rough puddings weren't in the mariner's code.

On and on crawled the pudding, puffing and bubbling and steaming. Over the road, down the lanes and into Pagwell Park. It ignored notices to keep off the grass. It banged on people's front doors. It climbed up and peered in at people's bedroom windows. And being peered at through your bedroom window by wild lemon and strawberry pudding is something you don't expect.

On and on it went. The London papers heard about it and sent reporters down, but they were immediately pudding-bound. But that didn't stop the papers reporting it. 'Pagwell Pudding Pandemonium,' said the *Daily Something*. 'Pudding helps itself to town,' said another paper. 'Pudding it on a bit thick,' said a third, reckoning it might as well be a bit funny.

But it wasn't a bit funny in Pagwell.

The fire brigade turned hoses on the pudding which made no difference. Then they squirted foam over it, but the pudding liked that. It thought it was cream. The Army came along and machine-gunned the pudding. It blew bits off it with shells and bombs, but the bits went on growing on their own.

The birds gorged themselves on the pudding and became so fat they couldn't fly and would have been easy victims for the Pagwell cats, but the cats were stuck fast in the pudding.

'Oh dear, oh dear!' cried the Professor. 'I ought to invent a pudding-destroying machine, but I can't get into my inventory to do it.'

'Bring out bulldozers!' shouted the Town Clerk, as the pudding surrounded the Town Hall. But bulldozers were no good. What they wanted were pudding-dozers and they didn't have any.

There was a slight setback for the prowling pudding when it reached the rhubarb plants in the vicarage garden, but that didn't stop it for long. It made an unauthorized detour through Colonel Dedshott's garden, outflanked the Catapult Cavaliers, flowed the wrong way up several one-way streets, and failed to give way to pedestrians at pelican crossings. If only there had been some pelicans there, they might have got rid of some of the pudding in their big beaks.

'We shall have to pass an anti-pudding bye-law,' said the Town Clerk as the Pagwell Council held an emergency meeting in an attic at the top of the Town Hall because the pudding was squatting in the rest of it.

'It must not be allowed to choke my drains,' said the Drains Councillor.

The Mayor, who was fed up with pudding, said nothing. He was due to retire the next day and reckoned the new Mayor could take on the pudding, and the best of Pagwell luck to him.

'Dear me, I really fear we shall have to evacuate the parish,' said the Vicar.

'Yes, indeed, I'm sure, sir,' said Mrs Flittersnoop, feeling very red in the face because she felt it was all her fault, but didn't see how it could be since it was the Professor's special ingredient that had started it all.

'For the first time in my, um, ah, life I must admit I am non-, er, plussed,' said the Professor. 'I have no idea what to do. No inventions occur to me.'

The pudding ramped on. It rode on the tops of single-decker buses, which is strictly against the traffic rules, and all the outer Pagwells were rapidly becoming Pudding Pagwells.

But ha! What was that sound in the distance? Was it native drums? Were the Didditupite Indians coming to the rescue? Had someone called out the guards?

No, no. But rescue looked as if it was coming.

Thump, thump, thump. The sound grew louder as it grew nearer. *Thump, thump, thump.* The people of Pagwell craned their necks out of their best bedroom windows and looked like a lot of unlikely cuckoo clocks.

Thump, thump, thump.

Then into view over the brow of a hill came an army. Not of soldiers, or marines, or air force personnel. It was an army of schoolboys.

Thump, thump, thump they marched, led by the Headmaster of Pagwell College. *Thump, thump.* Each boy carried a spoon at the slope and a plate under his left arm. *Thump, thump.*

'Charge!' shouted the Headmaster, and his glasses fell off into the pudding and were almost lost for ever.

Thumpetty, thumpetty, zuz, zim. The schoolboys attacked, plates at the ready, spoons waving.

And they set about the pudding as only schoolboys can. *Chump, champ, chomp, thump, thump, chump, chump.*

The pudding began to diminish. Soon half of Pagwell Park was clear.

'Up boys and at 'em!' shouted Colonel Dedshott, almost remembering what the Duke of Wellington said at Waterloo.

'Well I, am, ah, astonished!' gasped the Professor, waving his five pairs of spectacles.

Chump, chump. The schoolboys waded into the rampant pudding. But ha! The pudding sent reinforcements by way of Upper Pagwell. The battle raged fast and spongy. The air was thick with the clash of spoons on plates, the thump of pudding, the chump of scholastic jaws.

'We're gaining!' cried Mr Stinckz-Bernagh, the science master, making tests of the pudding which blew up slightly in his face.

Chump chump, bubble bubble, thump. The pudding battle raged.

Several schoolboys retired defeated. Half an acre of pudding overcame Form Five of Lower Pagwell Primary.

''Vast there!' shouted Commander Hardaport (Retired). 'The boys are losing!'

'Oh dear, my, um, ah, goodness!' groaned the Professor. 'If the pudding gets the better of the boys we are all, um, ah, done for. We shall be submerged in eternal pudding.'

The boys began to fall back. The pudding gathered itself and surged forward.

'I fear all is lost!' wailed the Vicar, saying all the prayers he could remember, but leaving out the bit about daily bread in case it was too much like daily pudding.

Then suddenly another sound came from the distance.

Pop, pop, popetty, pop zip, zip, zip.

And over another hill came an army of schoolgirls. They were armed to the teeth with spoons and plates, and led by Miss Frenzie of the Pagwell Publishing Company, who was brandishing a notebook in one hand and a wooden spoon in the other. She was closely followed by her secretary, Violet, who was bearing a garden trowel and a dustpan.

'Whoopee!' screamed the girls and they fell on the pudding, urged on by memories of school lunches and appetites stropped and sharpened by determined games of netball and horrific hockey.

The pudding battle surged on. The air was double thick with

flying pudding, leaping spoons and the clatter of teeth. Scraps of school songs mingled with scraps of pudding. There was certainly a good deal of scrapping. Three schoolboys ate two girls' helpings of pudding and were chased across the playing fields. The battle swayed this way and that. Then it swayed that way and this. Mrs Flittersnoop went to stay with her sister Aggie, but found the house full of pudding. Professor Branestawm hid in the Great Pagwell Library, but found pudding reading the books he wanted. Colonel Dedshott and the Catapult Cavaliers were bogged down in pudding, and the Vicar had pudding up his organ pipes.

Slosh, thump, chomp, chomp, burp. The battle reached its climax. Then it did it again. More climaxes were reached in this battle than in the Hundred Years' War.

But at last the frightful pudding was subdued, overcome, devoured and consumed, and all the schoolboys and schoolgirls had to be carried home because they were too full to walk.

The Pagwell mums had an easy week after that with no school lunches to prepare. The schools closed down for six days as the pupils were sleeping off the battle.

But Pagwell was saved. Not, it is feared, through any miraculous invention of the Professor's this time. In fact the Professor felt very red about the ears through having caused it all.

'Don't you ever do such a thing again, if you please, sir,' said Mrs Flittersnoop.

'No, indeed, I'm sure,' said the Professor meekly.

2

Automobile Ablutions

Doctor Mumpzanmeazle was busy washing his car. He found it a nice change from looking after patients. For one thing if it got spots on it they washed off quite easily. For another it never put its tongue out at him, and, for several more, it never called him out in the middle of the night because it was going to have a baby, didn't expect him to feel its pulse and didn't complain about its lumbago.

But all the same, washing it was harder work than washing patients because rather ruthless nurses did that at Pagwell Hospital, whereas Dr Mumpzanmeazle had to wash the car himself. *Slosh, slosh, rub, rub, rub, squeeze, trickle, squirt, slosh, rub.* Very tiring, but, thank goodness, not infectious.

'Ah, good, um, morning, Doctor,' said a voice and Professor Branestawm drew up in his own specially invented car, which not only looked as if it could do with a wash, but also as if it was quite likely to put its tongue out at you, come out in spots and complain about almost anything.

'Don't like this job much,' said the Doctor, leathering away like mad. 'Wish I could give the thing a pill or something instead of having to wash it.'

'I believe there is an, um, ah, car-washing depot in Pagwell,' said the Professor. He knew about it because they'd refused to let his car in on the grounds that they only washed cars, not infernal machines, and they were afraid the Professor's car might blow up in their faces.

'Yes, yes, I know,' said Doctor Mumpzanmeazle, squeezing windscreen-cleaning stuff out of a tube all over the place, 'but it's inconvenient to get to. One-way streets and all that. Besides it's closed on my day off. Why don't you invent one you can keep in the garage?'

'Ah,' said the Professor, who kept so many other things in his garage, including two beloved armchairs of Mrs Flittersnoop's that she couldn't bear to part with and couldn't find space for in the house, that there wasn't room for his car, let alone a car-washing thing.

'Well, I must be, um, ah, off,' said the Professor. 'I just stopped to say, er, er . . .' He found he'd forgotten what he'd stopped to say, started up his car, shot off in the wrong direction, made a U-turn in a no go area, went half way the wrong way up a one-way street, reversed into a milk cart and knocked over fifty coupons entitling you to a pair of trousers loudly marked 'Pagwell Dairy' if you ordered five pints more milk than you needed. Then he shot off towards Lower Pagwell, where he was going to collect Mrs Flittersnoop from her sister Aggie's and take her shopping.

'It's such a nice day, sir,' said Mrs Flittersnoop, when the shopping had cleared up, 'I thought we might go for a picnic in the country. I've brought a vacuum flask and some sandwiches.'

'Er, um, ah, yes, excellent idea!' said the Professor, and after getting lost five times, he and Mrs Flittersnoop finally arrived in a nice country sort of place full of grass, cows with what looked like maps of the world on them and very hearty rural smells.

'Why, look there, sir!' said Mrs Flittersnoop, pointing to a notice by a hedge. 'Self-Pick Strawberries. We could get some strawberries to have after our picnic, with some ice cream from that ice cream van over there.'

'Yes, yes, of course,' said the Professor, coming back from thinking out an idea for converting their bathroom into a private cinema. 'Give me your basket and I'll get the strawberries.'

The Professor found the strawberry-gathering business a bit frustrating because he thought 'Self-Pick' strawberries meant that they picked themselves and all you had to do was walk round with a basket and let the strawberries jump into it. After all, he had some self-pick apples on a tree in his garden. They used to pick themselves and drop on his head. But they didn't help him to discover the law of gravity because Isaac Newton had already done that. Instead they helped him to discover the law of getting out of the way of falling apples by sitting under an acacia tree, which didn't have self-pick things to fall on your head.

'Um, ah, most enjoyable,' he said, after Mrs Flittersnoop had picked the self-pick strawberries and got some self-get ice cream to go with them. 'Now, I, um, ah, fancy a cup of, er, tea.' He picked up the vacuum flask Mrs Flittersnoop had thoughtfully brought and poured himself out a cup of boiling water.

'Dear me,' he said. 'Really, Mrs Flittersnoop, people are always making fun of my being absent-minded and forgetting things, but this time it is you who have forgotten the tea!'

'Oh no, indeed, I'm sure, sir,' said Mrs Flittersnoop, taking a little box out of her picnic basket. 'I always fill the vacuum with boiling water and bring the tea bags to put in at the last moment. It makes the tea fresher, I always say, sir.'

'Um, ah, yes,' said the Professor, and he began to think of inventions again.

'Ha,' he said suddenly, spilling tea over his Continental Ripple Multi-Flavour Fruity Ice Cream. 'This self-pick strawberry business gives me an idea. Why not a self-washing motor car?'

'I don't think it would taste very nice,' said Mrs Flittersnoop, her mind still hovering round the strawberries.

'No, no, no, not to *eat*!' cried the Professor, waving sandwiches and spectacles about. 'I mean a car that washes itself to save you having to do it.'

'Yes, indeed, I'm sure, sir,' said Mrs Flittersnoop, as she couldn't think of anything else appropriate to say.

*

'The um, ah, principle is already established, Dedshott,' said the Professor to his friend Colonel Dedshott of the Catapult Cavaliers, who had been sitting in his dining-room winning the tenth battle of Pagwell for the seventeenth time with pepper pots, salt shakers, pots of marmalade and other military equipment.

'Yes, by Jove, what!' cried the Colonel, making a pincer movement with two pots of ginger marmalade on the vinegar bottle.

'The self-washing motor car is a natural development of the windscreen wiper,' said the Professor, waving his five pairs of spectacles about and losing the Colonel a skirmish with the salt shakers. 'You press a button, liquid is squirted on to the windscreen and windscreen wipers clean the glass. My idea is to develop this principle to, um, ah, cover the entire car.'

'Ha, yes, good idea, my word, what!' said the Colonel, reckoning that a car covered in windscreen wipers would be jolly popular with the traffic wardens because it would give them no end of places to put parking tickets.

'The idea might eventually be extended to self-cleaning tanks and artillery,' said the Professor, trying to get on the right side of the Colonel's military mind.

But the Colonel's military mind took a hasty left turn. He reckoned self-cleaning military equipment would be drastically unpopular with the Army, which always liked its soldiers to do plenty of spitting and polishing and shining things up nice and bright all ready for getting them lovely and muddy again. It kept the soldiers busy in peace-time when there weren't any enemies to fight.

'The general outlay would be something like this,' said the Professor, sweeping the battle of Pagwell on to the floor and starting to draw outrageous plans on the table-cloth.

'The, um, ah, motive power would of course be supplied by the car's engine,' he said, drawing four squiggles and ten squares.

'This would operate one or more, er, pumps, which would be supplied by a cleaning agent which I shall devise specially to remove all kinds of dirt and, um, er, stains without harming the paintwork.' He drew three more squiggles and several uncircular circles. 'Jets would be directed at various parts of the car body,' he went on, 'and by means of special electronically-controlled devices every part of the car would be cleaned, rinsed, dried and then polished off.' He polished off the rest of the table-cloth with symbols, devices, figures and lurid lines.

'Ha, my word, by Jove, jolly clever, what!' cried the Colonel, wishing he had a self-washing table-cloth.

Noises were coming from Professor Branestawm's inventory, which was quite usual. But what wasn't at all usual was that the windows, which were usually more opaque than the walls, were shining clear, and if it hadn't been for the clouds of high-octane steam you could have seen what was going on inside. Jets of bright green soapy water shot out in all directions. There were buzzings and gurglings and hissings.

Professor Branestawm was in the middlemost middle of inventing his incredible super-impossible, self-washing motor car.

Mrs Flittersnoop, who rather wished she had some self-washing dishes, was doing the dinner things when the Professor shot in covered in coloured soap bubbles and emitting steam from his ears.

'Success!' he cried, waving his spectacles about. They flew out of his hands and landed in the bowl of kind-to-your-hands, yet removes-all-trace-of-grease, washing-up liquid.

'I have done it!' he cried, dancing about. 'The world's first and only self-washing motor car is an accomplished fact.'

'Indeed, I'm sure, sir,' said Mrs Flittersnoop, wiping her hands on the kitchen towel and preparing for the worst.

Pausing only to ring up Colonel Dedshott, call over the fence to Commander Hardaport (Retired), send a message to the Vicar and write to the papers, the Professor grabbed Mrs Flittersnoop by the hand and rushed her out into the road.

There stood a motor car. Or, at least, what looked more or less like a motor car. It was actually a rather elderly second-hand one the Pagwell Bargain Price Superior Pre-Owned Car Company had let the Professor have as they couldn't find anyone short-sighted enough to buy it.

'What are all those little holes, by Jove?' asked Colonel Dedshott, who had arrived hot hoof on his horse in response to the Professor's call.

'How's the thing work?' asked Commander Hardaport (Retired), while the various other people the Professor had summoned to see his invention stood about waiting for things to happen, which they were pretty sure to do once the Professor's invention got going.

'Be-, um, ah, hold!' cried the Professor, throwing out his hands and knocking the Vicar's hat off. 'The unique and never before achieved self-washing car. You simply press this lever and *voilà*!'

Voilà it certainly was, *avec* trimmings, since we're being a bit French. Jets of boiling water shot out of the little holes in the car. Clouds of automobile steam arose. Soap suds of all colours flew about. Everybody got a free shampoo and their clothes washed. Noises occurred. Two rather new policemen, who were passing hurriedly by, ran round the corner and started writing in their notebooks. They found it difficult to describe what they'd seen, but felt it must be against the law.

The entire street looked like the world's washing day. Pink and blue fog covered everything. A strong smell of electronic cleaning was everywhere. Then the air cleared, the noises stopped and there was the car, polished and shining so bright that it hurt you to look at it.

'Marvellous, my word!' cried Colonel Dedshott, wiping his horse, which had been given a rather thorough shampoo by accident, with a spare dishcloth Mrs Flittersnoop had fetched.

'Could mean self-cleaning battleships, y'know,' said Commander Hardaport (Retired). 'No more swabbing decks and all that. Press button and warship cleaned for action. But bet Admiralty wallahs won't have it. Too easy for the crew, y'know. Make 'em soft.'

Mrs Flittersnoop thought soft sailors sounded rather attractive, but didn't like to say so.

'Now,' said the Professor, 'I propose to adapt my self-washing car principle to Doctor Mumpzanmeazle's car. It will, um, ah, give him more time to attend to his patients.'

The party dispersed to get dried off and the Professor went round to see the Doctor.

Doctor Mumpzanmeazle was once again washing his car. But this time he felt it would be a nice change to be attending to his patients. For one thing they never needed leathering down. For another they very rarely got mud on their bumpers. Their oil levels didn't need topping up and they didn't have to go through a Ministry of Thingummy test every year after they were three years old. He felt there was something to be said for patients, but, unfortunately, most of them were only too ready to say it for themselves.

'Ah, good, um, morning, Doctor,' said Professor Branestawm, arriving in a cloud of mixed dust, smoke and spectacles. 'I have good news for you!'

'Don't say good health has become infectious,' said the Doctor. 'That would be good news in a way, but it would put us doctors out of work.'

'No, no, no,' said the Professor, waving his hands. 'My good news is that you need not wash your car ever again. I have invented a method which can be applied to any car, enabling it to wash and polish itself. I shall be happy to adapt your car for that purpose.'

'Oh, ah, yes,' said the Doctor, talking a bit like the Professor for a moment. He wasn't quite sure whether the Professor's cure for car washing might not have undesirable side effects. But after thinking a moment he decided that even side effects were worth risking, if it avoided having to keep washing the car.

'All right, thank you very much,' he said. 'It so happens I am due for a holiday, so you can do the job while I'm away.'

Doctor Mumpzanmeazle was away rather longer than he expected because he caught a germ that was having a holiday in the same place. So the Professor had plenty of time to convert his car to the marvellous new Branestawm self-washing, self-polishing, keep-itself-clean model before he returned.

'While driving along you simply press this lever,' said the Professor, when he brought Doctor Mumpzanmeazle's adapted car back, 'and the car will wash itself. No trouble at all. Very useful if one runs into a thunderstorm or gets mud on the car. It will wash itself clean as it goes along.'

'Ha,' said Doctor Mumpzanmeazle and he set off, intending to drive to the clinic where he had rows and rows of patients waiting with their tongues hanging out to be prescribed fancy pills.

Halfway to the hospital the car went through a muddy puddle and the Doctor thought this was the time for it to wash itself, so he pulled the lever.

Whizz, swish, thrump, whizzle, swish, hiss. Steam and jets of coloured water and strong shampooing smells occurred and the car was clean in no time.

'Wonderful!' muttered the Doctor. He slowed down to take a corner and bang! Someone who was in more of a hurry to get to the clinic than he was, ran into the back of his self-washing car, didn't stop and shot off again.

'Good gracious!' exlaimed the Doctor, wondering if he was expected to treat injured cars as if they were injured people.

But Professor Branestawm's sensational self-washing car wasn't going to stand being bonked up the rear by impatient motorists. It shot off round the next corner, emitting jets of hot water, clouds of steam and more car-cleaning smells.

Doctor Mumpzanmeazle tried to stop it. He switched off the self-cleaning works, but the car took no notice. He put on the brakes, but the car took them off again. He changed gear, but the car changed back again. Down Pagwell High Street it raced, washing itself and all the parked cars it met. It went past a pedestrian crossing and shampooed the waiting pedestrians. A police car gave chase and overtook it, but it washed the police car out of the way and surged on. Pagwell streets, Pagwell shops and Pagwell people had bath night on Thursday morning for the first time in their lives.

'By Jove, there goes the Doctor in Branestawm's car!' cried Colonel Dedshott, who was cantering along with some of the Catapult Cavaliers. 'Out of control too, by Jove! After him!'

With swords waving and harnesses jingling, they galloped after the car.

Commander Hardaport (Retired) came out of a shop that sold ropes and binnacles and got it green, yellow and pink over the bows as the self-washing car shot by at a rate of knots.

Professor Branestawm came out of a side turning in his own car, received a shampoo and blow dry, and gave chase too.

All Pagwell was wringing wet and smelt of all the world's washdays. Even the Town Hall was covered in iridescent bubbles.

'I'll steer it towards the fire station!' cried Doctor Mumpzanmeazle, twiddling the steering wheel. 'They're used to jets of water and that sort of stuff. They'll be able to deal with it.'

But good gracious! The fire station was on fire! Outrageous and certainly against the bye-laws. And worse still all the fire engines were out! An electrical fault had set off the alarm, and while the fire engines were out looking for a fire that didn't exist, the electrical fault made one of its own at the fire station.

Oh, direful situation! Oh, tragedy! Oh, most irregular behaviour! Suppose there was a fire at the Town Hall, all the fire engines were out and the fire station was on fire? The Mayor's teapot might be destroyed. The new laws putting up the rates might be burnt. Worse still, suppose there was a fire at the Mayor's house? It didn't bear thinking about, and Doctor Mumpzanmeazle certainly didn't have time to think about it.

His self-washing car shot straight for the burning fire station. Into the flames it went, jets of hot water and smelly shampoo shot out right and left, and would have shot out in many other directions if there'd been any.

Hiss, hiss, splish, squish, roar, boom, slosh. The self-washing car attacked the flames as if they needed their faces washed. Clouds of steam, some pink, some green and some dirty, rose into the air. Hissings occurred. But at last the flames died down and the self-washing car stopped spouting coloured shampoo, cleaned its windows, polished its chromium plate and practically dusted off its hands at a job well done.

'It is rather difficult to decide', said the Mayor in his best bazaar-opening voice, 'whether to reward Professor Branestawm for inventing the machine that, although unintentionally, saved our fire station, or whether to reward Doctor Mumpzanmeazle, who was driving the car at the time and went into the fire at the risk of his life.'

The firemen were all for rewarding both of them because the fire station was rather severely scorched and had to be done up. That meant they had a few weeks' holiday while the fire brigades from the outer Pagwells took over the job until the Great Pagwell Fire Station was restored and ready for forms to be filled in stating where and when and why fires occurred and what action was taken.

At last the Mayor and the council decided to reward Doctor Mumpzanmeazle with a new car, a non-self-washing one just to be on the safe side. And they rewarded the Professor by ordering self-washing fire engines which would not only keep themselves bright and shining, but which could be relied on to put out fires quicker than the old kind and with much better smells.

'I am, um, er, ah, very glad', said the Professor, 'that my invention has proved to be of some public benefit and has also, um, ah, incidentally benefited Doctor Mumpzanmeazle by getting him a new car.'

The Doctor was delighted too. He still had to wash his car by sleight-of-hand, but then that was safer than having one of the Professor's inventions. His nice ordinary car wasn't likely to make him an unwilling understudy fireman, and spots were safer than flames.

3

Mrs Flittersnoop's Invention

Professor Branestawm had just finished a hearty breakfast of egg-on-waistcoat and instantly spilt coffee, when he found he'd left his reading glasses upstairs and needed them to read the *Pagwell Gazette*.

So he went up to get them, and on the way met Mrs Flittersnoop coming down. She had been doing the bedrooms and discovered that her polishing duster was down in the kitchen.

Later on the Professor had to come downstairs from changing into his lecturing suit for giving a talk at Pagwell College to get his cuff-links, which he thought he'd left in the dining-room, but which were actually on his dressing-table. So he had to go up again.

Meantime Mrs Flittersnoop was popping up and down the stairs, getting the washing together.

'These stairs are really getting me down,' she panted, climbing up them again.

'It, ah, seems to me that at the moment they are getting you up,' said the Professor, who liked to be very precise if he happened to think of it.

'It's nothing but upstairs downstairs, like one of those television programmes, sir, that I'm sure,' she said, bringing down an armful of towels and climbing up again for sheets and pillow-cases.

'It, um, ah, seems to me', said the Professor, beginning to feel an invention coming on, 'that whatever we need to have downstairs is always upstairs and, er, um, the things we want upstairs are invariably downstairs.'

'Yes, indeed, I'm sure, sir,' gasped Mrs Flittersnoop, going upstairs again after one of the Professor's socks that had got away on the last trip.

'Perhaps we should move to a bungalow,' murmured the Professor. 'Then there would be no upstairs.'

Mrs Flittersnoop tried to imagine the Professor with nothing upstairs and definitely failed.

'Or, um, ah, perhaps a flat,' went on the Professor. 'But then, if it was an upstairs flat we should still have stairs; but then, there would be a lift, unless it broke down, and we shouldn't have to come down unless we wanted to go out and when we were out, we should not need anything that was upstairs.'

'Oh no, sir, don't say we're going to move again!' cried Mrs Flittersnoop, stopping wringing a sheet to wring her hands. 'I remember the trouble we had last time, and what would you do about an inventory, sir? They don't have them in these high-rise flats, so I'm told.' The she suddenly clapped a hand to her forehead, which made drops of super-biological detergent run down her face, as her hands were wet.

'My goodness, sir, I'm sure!' she exclaimed. 'I believe I have an idea. An invention you might say, sir.'

Professor Branestawm said nothing.

What an outrageous situation! Mrs Flittersnoop inventing something. The very idea! Or indeed the very not-at-all idea. Surely professors' housekeepers couldn't go about inventing things. What was the world coming to? If that sort of thing was going to be allowed there was no knowing what would happen next. Pupils at schools might start getting their homework done in time instead of watching the telly. The television might go getting the weather forecast right. Buses might run to time, with room on them for people. Prices might go down instead of up, and inflation might explode backwards.

'Did you, um, ah, say you had an idea for an invention?' asked the Professor, getting his breath back and sorting his spectacles out.

'Well, not as you might say an *invention*,' said Mrs Flittersnoop, wiping the drops of detergent off her face with a second-best pillow-case, 'but I thought, sir, if I might make so bold, of a way to save so much running up and down stairs.'

The Professor sat down to listen in case Mrs Flittersnoop had been hit with a world-shaking idea that might go to his legs.

'I thought, sir,' said Mrs Flittersnoop, rather apologetically, 'that if we put on the bottom stair things that had to go up and on the top stair things that had to go down, we could then take them up or down as the case might be, if you follow me, sir, when we happen to be going up or down.'

Professor Branestawm's head began to go ever so slowly round and round, just as Colonel Dedshott's always did when he explained inventions to him.

Just then there was a knock at the door and Colonel Dedshott himself came in, medals and all.

'Ha, morning, by Jove, what!' he cried. 'Heard you were going to lecture at the College and thought I might come too and sort of back you up, you know. Keep order in class, what!'

'Well, er, thank you very much,' said the Professor. 'By all means come with me, I shall be, um, ah, delighted. But I don't think there is much chance of any, er, misbehaviour by the pupils as they are all girls.' Which showed how much the Professor knew about girls, or perhaps it didn't.

But Mrs Flittersnoop wasn't going to miss the chance of explaining her great and sensational staircase invention to the Colonel. And by the time she'd finished his head was going round at a fine rate of revs, even faster than the Professor's.

'Well of course it's a very good and practical idea of Mrs Flittersnoop's,' said the Professor, as he and the Colonel set off for the College. 'Leaving things on the stairs to be taken up or down whenever one has to go. Saves unnecessary journeys, which I seem to remember the Government used to want us to do, or was it to save electricity? But then saving up electricity means you need batteries to store it in, and the Government said nothing about supplying free batteries.'

'Ha, by Jove, no!' snorted the Colonel, who thought the idea of the Government supplying anything free, except ferocious guns and alarming aeroplanes, was slightly outrageous.

'But', went on the Professor, trying on various pairs of spectacles so as to arrange all five pairs in convenient order, 'Mrs Flittersnoop's idea still does nothing, I fear, to overcome the, um, ah, problem of needing something that is upstairs when you are downstairs and the other way round.'

'My word, no, what!' said the Colonel, who never worried much about things being upstairs or downstairs, because he simply sent his Catapult Cavalier butlers running smartly up or down stairs, as necessary, with their thumbs in line with the seams of their trousers and their eyes to the front.

When Professor Branestawm got back from Pagwell College, where he'd left the pupils a bit bewildered after lecturing them about the need for abolishing staircases in one-storey houses, he found one of Mrs Flittersnoop's aprons lying at the bottom of the stairs.

'Oh, ah, yes, of course,' he muttered, 'she wants that to go upstairs next time someone is going up.' And although he hadn't thought of going up, he picked up the apron and took it upstairs, just to be obliging.

But Mrs Flittersnoop had really thrown the apron downstairs to go in the washing and didn't want it taken upstairs at all.

'Now I, um, ah, wonder where she wants it put?' said the Professor to himself, as there was nobody else there to say it to. He folded the apron carefully the wrong way round and put it by the top of the stairs. 'Mrs Flittersnoop will know where she wants it,' he thought. Then, as it was a rather breezy day and Mrs Flittersnoop was rather a one for having all the windows open as much as possible, he thought he'd better put something on the apron to stop it blowing away. It was one of the Professor's thoughtful days.

'Ah, um, yes, the very thing,' he said. And he picked up the kettle that was kept on the upstairs landing for making early morning tea to save having to go downstairs to make it and then having to bring it up again. He put the kettle on the apron and went downstairs and out into the garden to try to think of an invention to make apples grow on gooseberry-bushes, so as to be nice and low down for picking instead of growing at the top of tall trees, where the best apples always seem to grow out of reach.

While he was out there Colonel Dedshott called to bring back the Professor's hat, which he'd left behind at the College and which had been rescued just in time before it was made into fancy tea-cosies and frightful slippers by some of the girls.

'You there, Professor, what?' called the Colonel. But he got no reply as the Professor was under a gooseberry-bush wondering why people said babies were found there, since he felt sure babies would find the place rather prickly.

'Hrrrmph,' said the Colonel, screwing up his moustache, and he went upstairs to see if the Professor was up there, but of course he wasn't. Then he saw the kettle and apron at the top of the stairs.

'Ha, my word!' he said, remembering what Mrs Flittersnoop had told him about her staircase invention. 'Things to go downstairs, eh. Better take 'em down on my way, what!'

So he carefully carried the upstairs kettle downstairs, together with Mrs Flittersnoop's apron, and put them on the kitchen table, dropping the Professor's hat at the bottom of the stairs without noticing.

'Ha, there you are, Branestawm!' he cried, seeing the Professor through the kitchen window. And he went out into the garden to tell him he'd brought back his hat.

At that moment Mrs Flittersnoop came back from shopping and saw the Professor's hat at the foot of the stairs.

'Now, why on earth does he want his hat taken upstairs?' she wondered. But knowing better than to wonder too much about why the Professor might want anything, she put the shopping on the hall table and took some striped toilet rolls, twopence off and five for the price of four if you took three, up to the bedroom. And she took the Professor's hat up with her and put it on his bed.

While she was in the bathroom putting the toilet rolls away and tidying things up by fishing the Professor's toothbrush out of the bath and unhooking his face flannel from the electric light, Commander Hardaport (Retired) arrived and got entangled in gardening conversation with the Professor and Colonel Dedshott, which then turned to inventing conversation and the Professor told the Commander about Mrs Flittersnoop's upstairs downstairs invention, but he got it a bit muddled.

Then they all went inside for a cup of something and the Commander saw Mrs Flittersnoop's shopping basket on the hall table.

'Ha, goods to be sent to the upper deck!' he cried and being helpful, as all sailors are trained to be after months and months of rushing up and down rigging, he carried the groceries upstairs and put them in the Professor's bedroom.

While Mrs Flittersnoop, who had come out of the bathroom, was wondering why the Professor wanted packets of cornflakes and jars of marmalade at a special price with a free book of knitting instructions for six labels and ten p postage in his bedroom, Professor Branestawm had gone out, forgetting to drink his cup of something, and was boasting to his friends all over Pagwell about Mrs Flittersnoop's wonderful invention.

'She gets it from me of, um, ah, course,' he said. 'Being intimately associated, as it were, with my, er, inventions, I have no doubt generates inventive inclinations in Mrs, um, Flittersnoop's mind.'

'But I don't quite understand', said the Vicar, 'how leaving things at the bottom or top of the stairs saves you going up for something you want downstairs or vice versa, as they say.'

'Um, ah, yes, of course,' said the Professor. 'That was my point exactly, but I really do not see any way of arranging for things to be both upstairs and downstairs at once.'

'Unless you have two,' said Maisie, one of the Vicar's twin daughters, or else it was Daisie, the other one.

'My dear young lady,' said the Professor, 'the fact that you have to have things upstairs and downstairs does very little to solve the, ah, problem.'

'I don't mean have *to*, I mean have *two*,' said Maisie, or was it Daisie?

The Professor's head began to go slowly round and he thought if the Vicar's twin daughters were going to start having ideas for inventions too, life was going to get a little complicated.

'I mean, why not have two of everything?' said Maisie (or Daisie). 'One upstairs and one downstairs.'

'Well,' said the Professor, 'we have two of those, but I hardly like to mention, um, ah, places like that in front of young ladies.'

'Oh, she doesn't mean loos!' said Daisie, or perhaps it was Maisie. 'We've got five of them in the vicarage and it doesn't save any work at all. In fact Mum has to keep dashing up and down stairs renewing the toilet rolls. She means have two vacuum cleaners, for instance, and keep one upstairs and one downstairs, then you don't have to carry them up and down.'

'Um, ah, yes,' said the Professor. 'But that is still not quite the same thing. Suppose, for instance . . .' He ticked a point off on one finger and shot his spectacles, which he was holding, under the vicarage sideboard. 'Suppose I want my book on the nuclear potentials of astro-dynamic forces when under the control of electronic impulses, and it is in my bedroom and I am in the sitting-room? There is no known way of getting it except by, um, ah, going upstairs.'

'But if you had *two* copies,' said Maisie and Daisie both at once, 'one could be in the bedroom and one in the sitting-room.'

But of course that wouldn't have worked because the Professor would have taken the sitting-room copy up to read in bed, and would have forgotten to bring it down next morning, so both books would have been upstairs and, when he wanted to look at one in the sitting-room, he'd still have to go upstairs.

'How about a lift?' said the Vicar, but just then Doctor Mumpzanmeazle called to enquire after the Vicar's cold, which had conveniently vanished in the night, and offered the Professor a lift home as the Professor had forgotten to bring his car with him.

Then, what with the Professor telling some people and the Vicar, Commander Hardaport and Colonel Dedshott telling others about Mrs Flittersnoop's invention, and what with those people telling their aunties and cousins and uncles and best friends about it, the whole of Pagwell began thinking furiously about the Professor's upstairs downstairs problem and amateur inventing broke out in all directions.

Commander Hardaport said the thing was to have a bo'sun's chair to hoist you up and save walking up the stairs. But Mrs Flittersnoop didn't take kindly to being hoisted upstairs, sitting on a skinny little bit of wood.

Mr Stinckz-Bernagh, the science master at Pagwell College, devised an ingenious lift that didn't need a hole in the ceiling to go up and down, but it took up so much space there was no room for any rooms.

Mr and Mrs Hokkibats, who thought running up and

down stairs was tremendous fun, invented a special staircase game in which you gained points if what you wanted was up when you went up, or down when you went down, but you had to go back and miss a turn if it was the other way round.

The Vicar promised to give uplifting sermons on Sundays, and Pagwell Council decided to send a severe note round, printed on purple paper, saying that no lift, elevator, moving stairway, escalator, conveyor belt, or funicular railway must be installed in any house, office, shop, building or other messuage unless plans in quadruplicate had been submitted to the council two years previously and permission obtained, which would not in any case be given, owing to the problem of traffic on the newly opened by-pass.

'This is really, um, ah, awful,' said the Professor, returning home and walking into the hall just in time to miss being hit by a heap of washing Mrs Flittersnoop had thrown downstairs. Then, seeing pillow-cases and sheets and shirts and socks lying about the foot of the stairs the Professor carefully gathered them all up and took them upstairs, only to be met by Mrs Flittersnoop with another armful of washing which she was about to throw downstairs.

'Oh dearie me, sir, indeed, I'm sure!' she said, seeing the Professor with the washing she'd previously thrown down. 'I don't want those brought back up until they're washed.' And she took them away from him and threw them downstairs.

The Professor staggered downstairs, leaving his hat, which had been knocked off by the washing, upstairs, and staggered into his inventory.

'I give up,' he groaned, collapsing on to a box, but uncollapsing very quickly as there were some spiky things on it. 'Here is Mrs Flittersnoop inventing an idea for saving one from going upstairs and downstairs unnecessarily. And as if that were not, um, ah, enough, her invention works quite well as long as nobody who does not understand it tries to interfere with it. Ha! That is just like my inventions. But again, ha! Mrs Flittersnoop's invention cannot really go wrong as there is no mechanism connected with it. And although I am a Professor of, um, er, ah,' he couldn't remember what he was a professor of, 'I am quite, er, unable to devise an invention that will enable one to get things from upstairs when one is downstairs, without going up, or the other way round.' He shook his head and spectacles flew about. 'So the dreadful situation is that here am I, Professor of, er, um, ah, whatever it is, beaten at my own, er, game by my own housekeeper. I shall never be able to lift my head again.'

He leant miserably forward, hit his head on the bench and found he certainly couldn't lift it again as he'd laid it in some rather sticky instant glue he'd invented last week.

But fortunately Mrs Flittersnoop arrived with a cup of nice strong tea and got him prized off the bench and cleaned up. And she left him drinking his tea and with his brains going like twenty-four enthusiastic computers trying to invent a specially shattering invention to save himself from the disgrace of being out-invented by his own housekeeper.

And as for Mrs Flittersnoop, she finished the laundry and put it tidily at the foot of the stairs, had a cup of tea herself, then got on with the downstairs housework, leaving the washing to be taken upstairs next time she went. It made life a great deal easier, or would have done as long as the Professor was too busy inventing to help her.

4

Press-Button Shopping

Professor Branestawm was furious. He didn't often get furious, but this time he was. He clashed his spectacles, he gnashed his teeth, he stamped about.

'I, er, um, ah, pah!' he snorted.

It was all the fault of the Great Pagwell Bank. Not that they'd made any difficulties about letting him have money. Absolutely on the contrary. They'd made it too easy for everyone to get money, even when the bank was shut.

Yes, most dire and dreadful thing, the bank had actually invented a money-paying-out machine. You just pressed buttons and the money you wanted came out, as long as you first put in a special card. Highly ingenious. Oh dear, yes, but highly un-what's-its-name as far as Professor Branestawm was concerned. How dare banks go inventing machines? How absolutely dare they trespass on the Professor's preserves. He didn't trespass on theirs, did he? He didn't accept money deposits and pay interest on them. He didn't issue cheque books and stand behind bars weighing up money. No wonder he was furious when he saw the machine outside the Pagwell Bank.

'Disgraceful!' he cried to Mrs Flittersnoop when he got home. 'Banks have no right to go inventing machines. That is my job as a Professor of, er, thingummy. Oh, I know you invented an invention, Mrs Flittersnoop,' he added hastily, 'but that was just an idea for not going up and down stairs so often. It wasn't a *machine*. And anyway,' he smiled at Mrs Flittersnoop and his spectacles went crooked, 'you are one of the family so to speak, so that doesn't count.'

Mrs Flittersnoop wasn't absolutely sure she wanted to be one of the Professor's family, but she just said, 'Yes, indeed, I'm sure, sir,' and took away a cup of coffee just in time for the Professor not to bring his fist down on it. But he brought his fist down on a jam tart instead and stamped off to the bank again with it still sticking to him.

'It won't, um, ah, do, you know,' said the Professor to the bank manager. 'Banks can't go inventing machines. And suppose it goes wrong? Machines do, you know.'

'It has,' groaned the bank manager. 'Three times this morning and twice yesterday. Some of my customers were rather offended at what the machine said to them.'

'You must stop it at once and I will invent a money machine for you, if you must have one,' said the Professor, scraping the jam tart off into the bank manager's in-tray. He tipped it into the waste-paper basket, where it lay earning no interest whatsoever.

'No, no, my dear Professor,' said the bank manager. 'I think our machine is quite adequate. No doubt it will settle down. It's just that people aren't used to using it and they make mistakes.'

'It is you who made the mistake, inventing the machine in the first place,' snorted the Professor. 'I shall show you I am not a man to be trifled with. I shall invent a rival machine for shoppers which will put yours in the shade,' and he stamped out, leaving the bank manager in such a dither he had to go and count a lot of other people's money to make himself feel better.

Mr Pryce-Rize of the Pagwell Supermarket was delighted when the Professor explained his idea for a shopping machine.

'Terrific, my dear Professor!' he cried, knocking two p off a jar of raspberry jam and knocking five jars of rather viscous marmalade off a shelf in his excitement. 'It will mean people can shop after we are closed. It will save queues at the pay desks. It will be better than your floating supermarket because we shall not have the River Pag Controllers to worry us.'*

They shook hands and the Professor went home without taking advantage of any of the breath-taking-money-saving-limited-time offers that leered at him on the way out.

'Mrs Flittersnoop,' he called, as he came in at the kitchen door because he'd forgotten his front door key.

'Oh!' exclaimed Mrs Flittersnoop. 'You did startle me, I'm sure, sir.' She'd have dropped a bowl of cake mixture if she'd been holding one, but thank goodness she wasn't, as Mrs Flittersnoop's cake mixture was very tenacious and would have been difficult to detach from the floor.

'I beg your pardon,' said the Professor, putting his hat on the stove, but Mrs Flittersnoop snatched it up again before it could get over-cooked. 'I am going to invent a machine for people to do their shopping, so that they can shop when the shop is shut and don't have to wait in queues to pay, which they couldn't do if the shop was shut, you follow me?'

'Yes, indeed, I'm sure, sir,' said Mrs Flittersnoop, wiping her hands on her apron and making up her mind this was going to be another of those days.

'Come into the inventory,' said the Professor. 'I shall need your advice as to the kind of, er, groceries and other things shoppers wish to purchase.'

Then began a piece of inventing such as Mrs Flittersnoop had never known before and certainly hoped to escape knowing again.

The Professor asked questions, made notes, constructed models, altered and revised them, took them to bits, rebuilt them, asked more questions, didn't listen to the answers, couldn't find the long-nosed pliers and lost his spectacles among the files.

After inventing like this for some time, Mrs Flittersnoop gave

* see *Professor Branestawm Round the Bend*

up helping and retired to make cups of tea. Then Colonel Dedshott arrived, just in time to have his head made to go round and round as the Professor explained his invention.

'It is an idea I got from some absurd machine they have at the bank,' said the Professor. 'You just press buttons and it gives you money.'

'By Jove! Jolly good, what!' said the Colonel, who wouldn't have minded pressing a lot of buttons for money as he was sometimes pressed for it a bit himself.

'Banks, in my opinion', went on the Professor, 'should confine themselves to, ah, er, to that is to say they shouldn't invent machines. I told the bank manager so, and I am now inventing a machine that will show the bank where it, um, ah, gets off.'

The Colonel, who knew where to get off his horse at the bank, didn't quite see why the bank needed showing where to get off, as it was already there. But he knew better than to say so.

'This system of pressing buttons to obtain articles', went on the Professor, 'is capable of much interesting and intricate development. I am arranging a dial-your-grocery system which is more efficient than "pick and pay" or "pay as you earn" or "serve yourself" or any of the other methods now in, er, vogue.'

'Ha, my word, yes,' said the Colonel, sitting down on a box while his head did unmilitary about-turns and started going round anti-clockwise.

'It's very simple,' said the Professor, pointing to no end of highly complicated pieces of machinery. 'When this is erected outside the supermarket, all a customer has to do is spell out what he wants and the machine will deliver it. No hunting on the shelves for things the supermarket people have, um, ah, moved to a different place. No waiting in queues to pay for the goods. And', the Professor wagged a finger, 'you can buy things even when the shop is shut.'

'Wonderful, by Jove!' grunted the Colonel, who was never

very keen on buying things in shops even when they were open, as the lady assistants scared him a bit.

Getting the Professor's shopping machine assembled outside the Pagwell Supermarket was an operation slightly less dangerous than the battle of Agincourt, took rather less time than a trip to the moon, and didn't involve quite so many people as the building of the pyramids. But it ran all these notable events a close second.

First of all the machine was so large it had to be brought to the supermarket in bits. Then people had to stand guard over the bits in case they were stolen or damaged, while more bits were brought along. This caused a nice traffic jam in the High Street while the stuff was unloaded and a rather over-enthusiastic traffic warden gave a ticket to the Chief Policeman for stopping his car on quadruple yellow lines, which mean not only that you mustn't stop there, but that you have no right to be in a car at all.

Then bits of the supermarket had to be pulled out to make room for the machine. Notices were put up inside the supermarket apologizing for any inconvenience caused, but whether the customers accepted the apologies nobody knows.

Then the work of erecting the machine went on all night with clangs and bangs and shouts of 'A bit more to you, Les,' and 'Hold 'er up there, Jim,' and 'Where's me flowering spanner?' and other industrial talk.

People complained that they couldn't sleep, but the Professor pointed out that the noise was no more than that of a jumbo jet passing overhead, which happened several times a day and night, usually when you were on the telephone or had just got to sleep.

At last the great Branestawm Shopping Machine was fully installed and ready for action. The Mayor was invited to dial the first order, but said he'd rather not as he had a grocery shop of his own which he couldn't leave unattended. So Mrs Flittersnoop

TEA
TEA
TEA
£1·00
WINDOW
ALPHABET KEYS
NUMBERED KEYS
WEIGHTS MEASURES
EMPTY BASKETS
TOTAL
MONEY

was chosen as representative of a typical shopper, which she didn't think she was, and very likely wasn't, to sort of launch the machine.

The Professor stood by with explanations which were hardly needed as the machine did all the explaining necessary itself. There was a notice on it which said: 'Dial the name of the article required on the alphabetical keys. Then dial the number or quantity required on the numbered keys and those marked with weights and measures. When you have completed your order press the key marked Total. The amount due will appear in the window at the top of the machine and a drawer will open. Place the money in the drawer, close it and pull the lever. Your order will then be delivered ready for you to take away.'

'It all seems very nice, I'm sure, sir,' said Mrs Flittersnoop nervously. She approached the machine with her shopping list in one hand and the first finger of the other pointing out ready for key-pressing.

The assembled crowd of housewives, young girls and their boy friends, spare policemen and Mr Pryce-Rize of the Pagwell Supermarket all applauded, except for the policemen, who weren't sure whether applauding was legal while on duty.

Mrs Flittersnoop pressed keys, spelling out 'PLUM JAM', and pressed the 1 key. The she spelt out 'GRANULATED SUGAR KILOS $\frac{1}{2}$' followed by 'TEA BISCUITS GRAMS 250' and 'LEMONADE BOTTLES SMALL 6'. She pressed the Total button and the amount appeared in the window. She put the exact money in the drawer that had opened, closed the drawer and pulled the lever.

There were whirrings, clicks and buzzes. Things seemed to be going round rapidly and slowly both at once. Then there was an extra loud clang, a door opened and out slid a trolley basket with Mrs Flittersnoop's order neatly stacked in it. On the trolley there was another notice which said: 'When you have unloaded the trolley bring it back and place it in the empty compartment at the left of the machine.' The notice then added the warning: 'Trolleys not returned within two hours will emit a high-pitched scream as a safeguard against theft.'

'Well, I never!' exclaimed Mrs Flittersnoop, and there was a rush for the machine by the other shoppers who wanted to try it themselves.

'Most satisfactory, excellent, my dear Professor,' said Mr Pryce-Rize. 'I'm getting customers from other shops because people enjoy playing with the machine, and it saves my staff a lot of work.'

But, of course, a Branestawm invention wasn't going to let people have things all their own way, never mind how many lettered and numbered keys they pressed.

On the second day after it was installed a lady who wanted a sponge cake for tea dialled 'SPONGE 1' and got a large bath sponge.

Two days later another shopper wanting a nice pudding dialled 'CHOCOLATE MOUSSE,' but left out one 's' and got a little brown, sweet mouse. And another lady got a toy dog instead of the Chinese food she wanted when she dialled 'CHOW CHOW'.

Some of the shoppers weren't so hot at spelling, but the machine did its worst to oblige.

Someone who wanted lettuce got a lot of envelopes with saucy messages in them. Another shopper who wanted minced beef to make shepherd's pie got a roll of peppermints, while a request for steak produced a long thick wooden stick.

Miss Frenzie of the Pagwell Publishing Company, who was immersed in another of her frantic recipe books, came hurtling along and tried to get a packet of cornflour, but the machine misunderstood her and gave her a little blue plastic daisy.

Mrs Trumpington-Smawl arrived with a shopping list three yards long and ordered so many high-class and expensive groceries the machine ran out of trolleys and began firing parcels at her.

She was so annoyed at this that she dialled a ticking off complaint on the machine, to which the machine replied with an extremely rude word in the totalling window.

'Disgraceful!' snorted Mrs Trumpington-Smawl. She dialled a severe reply and got a very insulting answer.

Just then the Vicar came up, listened carefully to what Mrs Trumpington-Smawl had to say, read what the machine had said to her and got so confused that in trying to dial 'INSTANT COFFEE' he got mixed up and the machine gave him incense and a packet of toffee.

The Vicar dialled 'BEHAVE YOURSELF!', and the machine answered 'GET LOST' and delivered an out-of-date map to help him.

The Vicar lost his cool and delivered a kick at the machine, which retaliated with a 2p-off-packet of biscuits well smashed up.

'Disgraceful!' cried the Vicar, attacking the machine with his umbrella.

The machine let fly with cut-price bananas.

Colonel Dedshott arrived and tried to help tame the machine, but it put out complicated military orders and gave him a jar of military pickle.

The Colonel and the Vicar were joined by Commander Hardaport (Retired) and between them they got the machine in such a tiz it started sending out trolley loads of unwanted groceries of all kinds into the High Street traffic.

Then Mr Pryce-Rize got on the telephone to the Professor.

'Come at once, Professor,' he begged. 'Your machine has gone berserk. The High Street is in turmoil.'

Professor Branestawm arrived on the scene just in time to be given half a hundredweight of breakfast cereal. Mr Pryce-Rize came panting up, waving his arms.

'I, um, ah, think it needs some slight adjustment,' said the Professor. He twiddled some wheels on the machine which promptly called him an impolite name and gave him two empty lemonade bottles and a tin of drain un-stopper.

'No, no, no, no!' cried Mr Pryce-Rize. 'Don't adjust it! Stop it! I don't want it.'

'But I thought it had been such an, um, ah, success,' said the Professor, dodging a jar of peanut butter.

'Yes, yes, but too successful,' wailed Mr Pryce-Rize. 'People like the machine so much they're forming longer queues at the machine than they did in the shop. My cashiers have nothing to do. They're knitting woolly jumpers and learning to play the bassoon, in my time. Get rid of the thing, *please*, Professor.'

'Oh, ah, well,' said the Professor. But by this time the Colonel, the Vicar, Commander Hardaport and a few spare policemen had at last managed to get the better of the machine and it was in bits across the High Street.

'Well I think it's a pity, sir,' said Mrs Flittersnoop to the Professor later. 'It did save having to hunt for the things you want and these supermarkets do keep shifting things about, I'm sure, sir.'

So that was the end of the Professor's wonderful shopping machine. Mr Pryce-Rize got his cashiers off their bassoons and knitted jumpers and Professor Branestawm took his machine to pieces and made it into typewriters for deserving estate agents' secretaries.

5
The Vicarage Tree

'It will have to come down,' said the Vicar of Pagwell, looking up.

'It seems a pity,' said Professor Branestawm.

The spire of Pagwell Church said nothing, and didn't even look down as that is rather difficult for church spires to do.

But, of course, it wasn't the church spire the Vicar wanted down. It was a slightly enormous tree growing beside the church tower. Its topmost branches were poking into the belfry and trying to ring Grandsire Triples on the bells, while the bell-ringers were trying to ring Stedmans. The lower branches were scraping against the stained glass windows and making them stained in the wrong way. The roots were creeping into the crypt. And, on top of all that, the tree was keeping the sun out of the vicarage, a nice old English house with French windows, Venetian blinds, Swiss balconies and an Indian veranda. It also kept the sun off the lawn, which was apt to make vicarage garden parties a bit murky.

'The difficulty is', said the Vicar, 'how to get the tree down without damaging anything. My neighbour has a very large greenhouse and I shouldn't like any of the glass to get broken. Then there is the church itself. If the tree fell the wrong way . . .'

'Um, ah, yes, of course, quite,' said the Professor, his brains whizzing round like mad. 'I must, um, ah, invent some way of getting the tree down safely. The usual method, of course,' he waved his spectacles and one pair flew up into the tree like an impossible sparrow, 'is to climb up and cut the tree down bit by bit from the top.'

'Ha, yes, unlike your flagstaff-painting method which started at the bottom,* I believe,' said Commander Hardaport (Retired), who had just rolled up with a telescope under his arm.

'Ha! What's that up on the yard-arm?' he grunted, focusing his telescope on the Professor's tree-bound spectacles. 'Looks like a pair of your spectacles, Branestawm. Better get 'em down!'

He put the telescope on the ground and started to climb the tree. Up and up he went, as if the tree were the mast of a ship, only it was a bit more complicated because it had branches in more places than masts have yard-arms. At last he reached the spectacles, but found he was jammed between two thick branches and couldn't get down again.

'Below there!' he shouted. 'I'm shanghaied up this blessed thing. Get help, below!'

'Yes, yes, don't move!' shouted the Vicar. He rushed into the vicarage and telephoned for the fire brigade. But they were already busy at a fire elsewhere and before they could arrive, Colonel Dedshott rode up and immediately, with great gallantry, insisted on climbing up to the Commander's rescue. It wasn't too difficult as he had a start, being already on top of his large horse. Soon he reached the Commander, but found himself on the wrong side of the trunk.

'Ha! By Jove! Have to get round the other side,' he grunted.

Then he got stuck and Professor Branestawm, with the help of some passing scouts, two very short ladders and a lot of rope, managed to get himself to the top of the tree, where he was too high to reach either the Colonel or the Commander. The scouts climbed up to help, but they got stuck too.

Mrs Flittersnoop's cat came walking sedately by, climbed the tree very elegantly, sniffed at the various people in the branches, didn't think much of them, climbed down again and went home

* see *Professor Branestawm Up the Pole*

to see if there was a saucer of milk going.

Then a wind sprang up. The tree waved from side to side. The upper branches rang unauthorized and unheard-of peals on the church bells.

The organist, who was in the middle of choir practice, stopped playing so that he could hear the noise, and a clutch of choirboys in nice white surplices came surging out. They joined the scouts and soon the vicarage tree looked like a Christmas tree with scouts and choirboys dotted all over it, the Colonel and the Commander hung up like peculiar presents and Professor Branestawm at the very top of the tree like an incredible fairy.

'Oh dear, dear me,' moaned the Vicar, wondering what sort of prayers to say to whom to get people down from trees.

Miss Frenzie arrived with her secretary, Violet, and an assortment of schoolchildren who were studying botany and immediately climbed the tree as part of their lesson.

Of course with all those people up the tree it looked quite likely to come crashing down without any further help. The man from next door came rushing out waving his arms and shouting, 'Mind my greenhouse! Glass! Fragile! Danger! I shall hold you responsible for any damage, Vicar.'

But the tree didn't come down, and, thank goodness, the fire brigade came up at last. They put up a terrific ladder that extended itself as if it meant to get to the moon and firemen shot up it, rescuing the choirboys and schoolchildren and Commander Hardaport (Retired) and Colonel Dedshott, but not before a rather young and enthusiastic fireman had turned a hose on the Commander and washed him down as if he were a deck on his own ship.

Finally the Professor himself was rescued.

'Oh, ah, um, thank you very much,' he said. Then he looked up and saw that his spectacles were still up the tree. But before a spectacle-rescuing fireman could get up the ladder, an enterpris-

ing blackbird snapped up the spectacles and flew off with them.

'After him!' shouted Colonel Dedshott, drawing his sword but remembering just in time that he couldn't fly. The blackbird found the spectacles weren't eatable and didn't fancy them as furniture for its nest, so it dropped them in Mrs Flittersnoop's lap while she was peeling potatoes, and she brought them back to the Professor with a piece of potato peeling still hanging on one end, as she was in rather a hurry.

'Oh, ah, um, well, that seems to be everything satisfactorily settled,' the Professor said.

'No, no, Professor,' protested the Vicar. 'The tree, my dear sir, the tree. We still haven't thought of how to get it down.'

'Begging your pardon, Vicar,' said the Chief Fireman, raising his helmet and a packet of sandwiches he'd brought in case of a fire being a long one fell out, 'but if it's a matter of cutting down this here tree I think we can manage that, sir. What with our ladders we can easily get up at it. All we need is something to cut it with, and I don't fancy as our fire hatchets would be quite up to it.'

'Ha,' said Professor Branestawm. 'This is where I think we can co-er-operate. I will invent a branch-cutting machine which your firemen can use from their ladders.'

'Right you are, sir,' said the Chief Fireman, putting his sandwiches on his head and covering them carefully with his helmet. 'You do be letting me know when your branch-cutting machine be ready and we'll be along with the ladders.'

'Excellent, excellent,' said the Vicar.

Some time later, after the emergence from Professor Branestawm's inventory of branch-cutting machinery noises and cups of tea, coffee and cocoa that Mrs Flittersnoop had put through the window and collected later after the Professor had forgotten to drink them, the Professor came out with his machine.

It looked rather like an electric toothbrush for the Loch Ness monster, only it had teeth instead of bristles. It also had wheels and gears and levers and starting buttons, and as many other things as the Professor had managed to invent into it, including a pair of Mrs Flittersnoop's knitting needles that she couldn't for the life of her think what had become of.

The Professor called on the Vicar. The Vicar called the fire brigade, who came in a frantic rush, but became unfrantic when they found it wasn't a fire. Then the Chief Fireman, with his helmet strapped on nice and tight as there were no sandwiches in it this time, got ladders up the tree, firemen up the ladders, and the Professor's machine up with them.

Buzz, buzz, whiz, poppetty bang, bong, creeeeeeeeeek, crash. Down came the topmost branch of the tree, well clear of Mr Next-door's greenhouse, but splash in the middle of the vicarage duckpond. Fortunately the ducks were on holiday in the river.

Boppetty, bang, creeeek, crash. Down came another branch, and another and another. The tree grew shorter and smaller contrary to all the laws of nature, but there's no time to consider the laws of nature when vicarage trees have to be cut down without damaging next-door men's greenhouses.

Soon there was nothing left of the tree but the stump and what looked like fifteen thousand branches that filled the vicarage garden and overflowed into the road.

'Dear me,' said the Vicar. 'I had no idea there was so much of it.'

'You'll have to move these here branches,' said a passing policeman to the Vicar, not raising his helmet. This wasn't because policemen aren't as polite as chief firemen, but because policemen don't raise their helmets while on duty in case criminals bash them over the head while they're doing it. And anyway, the policeman had a nice pork pie in his helmet that he was taking home for lunch. Helmets can be very useful things.

'Oh dear,' said the Vicar. Getting rid of the tree now it was down looked like being even more difficult than when it was up. But fortunately the scouts, who'd been up the tree when it was up, knew how to deal with it now it was down. They arrived with trek carts and carted the pieces of tree away to cut up into logs for old-age pensioners to keep warm during the winter.

But the Vicar's troubles weren't over yet.

The stump of the tree was still there, with its roots trying to creep into the crypt.

'We shall never be able to dig that out,' he said.

But Professor Branestawm, who hadn't recovered from seeing his wonderful branch-cutting machine actually work without giving any trouble or attacking anybody, reckoned if he could do that he could invent a way of disposing of the tree stump. He wasn't going to be stumped by it, in fact.

'We shall blast it out!' he said, clamping all his spectacles firmly together and putting them in his pocket.

'Blast it?' said the Vicar, going rather red in the face as he felt that wasn't quite the sort of thing a Vicar should say. 'You mean with explosives, Professor? I feel that would be most unwise. The noises would upset the neighbours and the shock of the explosion would damage Mr Next-door's greenhouse.'

But Professor Branestawm calmed the Vicar's fears.

'I shall use my special noiseless explosive,' he said. 'I invented it for the Army so that they could attack the enemy without the enemy knowing it. Nobody will be annoyed. And as for Mr, um, ah, Next-door's greenhouse, you may safely leave it to me, Vicar. I shall devise a method of blasting the tree stump out without the slightest danger to the glassware.' And he went off leaving the Vicar not knowing whether to be glad he was going to be rid of the tree stump, or absolutely terrified that the Professor was going to do something extra disastrous.

*

'Er, ah, now,' said the Professor. 'Stand well back everybody while I detonate my special noiseless explosive and remove the Vicar's stump.'

Everybody stood well back, and the Vicar felt the Professor's reference to his tree stump made him feel rather as if he were at the dentist's.

'Just like war-time, my word,' grunted Colonel Dedshott. 'Dealing with unexploded bombs, doncherknow.'

'More like floating mines,' growled Commander Hardaport (Retired), who always felt the Navy should have one over on the Army whenever possible.

'Mind my greenhouse!' shouted Mr Next-door over the fence.

The Professor bent down over a little box arrangement, twiddled wheels, pulled levers and pressed a button.

There was a most tremendous burst of silence that couldn't be heard for miles around. Birds didn't rise out of the surrounding trees, as they're supposed to do when explosives go off, but the tree stump leapt into the air and split into little bits that showered down all over the lawn. Mr Next-door's precious greenhouse remained unharmed. Not so much as the tiniest crack in any of the glass.

'Bless me!' said the Vicar.

'Jolly good, Branestawm, by Jove!' cried Colonel Dedshott, twirling his moustache.

'Roger!' shouted Commander Hardaport, which, according to the telly, is what sailors always shout when they agree with something.

But out from next door rushed Mr Next-door in a very un-noiseless temper. He was shouting and waving one hand, while in the other he carried a pot with a geranium in it. And the flower had broken and was hanging down.

'You clumsy lot!' he shouted. 'Look what you've done! Ruined one of my geraniums. I hold you responsible, Vicar.'

While the Vicar was calming Mr Next-door with promises of a new geranium and an invitation to the next vicarage tea party, Professor Branestawm and the others collected the bits of tree stump and had a look into the large hole it had left.

'What's that down below?' cried Commander Hardaport (Retired), pointing into the hole.

'By Jove, it's buried treasure!' cried Colonel Dedshott.

Professor Branestawm grabbed a spade and jumped into the hole, spectacles and all. He flung out shovelfuls of earth all over the Colonel and the Commander. Then he flung out something else.

Thump. It was half a vase.

Another thump, three quarters of a dish.

Thumpetty, thump. Several complete bowls and two thirds of another vase.

'Good gracious!' exclaimed the Vicar. 'Who can have been burying all this broken china in the vicarage garden?'

'Romans,' said Professor Branestawm. 'Ancient Romans, although, of course, they may not have been very ancient when they left these things here. Pagwell', he went on, waving spectacles about in lecturing attitudes, 'was an Ancient Roman settlement. Originally it was Pagwellanium. This is a most, um, ah, interesting archaeological find.'

'But', protested the Vicar, 'they've already found Ancient Roman remains in Pagwell. I know about that. How is it these have remained undiscovered during recent excavations?'

'Chaps wouldn't go digging up the vicarage garden, me dear Vicar,' grunted Commander Hardaport (Retired).

'Ha, no, by Jove, what!' agreed Colonel Dedshott.

'Well,' said the Professor. 'Never mind why these valuable relics haven't been found before. We have them now. It is a great piece of luck for you, Vicar. We can sell them to the Pagwell Museum and get enough money for you to um, er, ha. . . .'

'Build a new church hall, have the organ tuned, have the bells re-hung, cure the rising damp in the crypt, provide kneeling cushions for the congregation, mend the roof, regild the weathercock, straighten the steeple . . .' chanted the Vicar eagerly.

So the bits of Roman pottery were carefully gathered in. More were discovered and dug out. At last there were several scout trek cart-loads of Ancient Roman pottery, including a not very ancient ginger beer bottle, all of which they took along to the Museum.

The Curator of the Pagwell Museum looked at it all. He looked at Professor Branestawm. He looked at the Vicar.

'We don't want it,' he said.

Professor Branestawm looked back at the Museum man. He looked at him first through one pair of glasses, then through another and finally through all at once.

'You don't want them?' he said. 'You don't want these unique, valuable, rare Ancient Roman relics?'

'No,' said the Museum man. 'We certainly don't. The place is stuffed full and a half of unique, valuable, rare Ancient Roman relics. Every time anyone digs a hole in Pagwell they find unique, valuable, rare Ancient Roman relics. They keep bringing them to us and we can't take them. Go and bury them again, and thanks very much.'

He closed the door slowly and politely and went in to have a non-unique, not very valuable and certainly not rare, cup of coffee and a not too ancient bun.

Professor Branestawm waved his hands. The Vicar waved his. The Colonel and the Commander shook their heads and made military and naval noises.

'What are we going to do with them?' asked the Vicar.

Then Professor Branestawm had one of his ideas. Not, thank

goodness, a world-shattering explosive idea for an invention guaranteed to lay waste half the countryside, but a nice, tame, well-behaved idea.

'We'll turn that hole the tree stump came from into an Ancient Roman sunken garden,' he said. 'It will be a great, um, ah, attraction for your garden parties, Vicar.'

And that was what they did. With the help of the scouts and a few friends of Mrs Flittersnoop's who were handy with spades, rakes and cement, they made an Ancient Roman sunken garden, paved with bits of Ancient Roman pottery and surrounded most decoratively with Ancient Roman urns, some whole and some mended. And at the entrance to it they erected a nice modern Ancient Roman sign that said S.P.Q.R., which could be said to stand for Surplus Pottery Quarried from the Romans, although, of course, it didn't.

6

The Professor's Um-ah-brella

'It's coming on to rain,' said Mrs Flittersnoop.

'Um, ah, er, yes,' said Professor Branestawm.

He'd gone out shopping with Mrs Flittersnoop, which seems an unlikely thing for the Professor to do. But then Professor Branestawm was always very likely to do unlikely things. He wanted to study the reaction of shoppers to the special offers made by shops and supermarkets in regard to their effect on inflation, if any, and the prevalence of bargains offered at not much more than the ordinary price.

'It's coming on to rain,' said Mrs Flittersnoop again. 'You'd better put your umbrella up, Professor.'

'Um, ah, er, yes,' said the Professor. He put down two plastic bags, one shopping basket, three awkwardly shaped parcels and a string bag, so as to have a hand free to put up his umbrella.

But he hadn't got his umbrella.

'Oh, dearie me,' said Mrs Flittersnoop, trying to rearrange three coloured plastic bags, a cardboard carton and her knitting, which she'd brought so as not to waste time in case she had to wait in a queue. 'I know you brought it because I said you'd better bring yours as it's bigger than mine and would do for both of us, if you remember, sir?'

'Um, ah, yes, indeed, I'm sure,' said the Professor, talking like Mrs Flittersnoop. 'But I haven't got it now. I must have left it in a shop.'

But which shop?

They'd been to no end of shops, plenty of supermarkets, one or two department stores, the shoe repairer's, the cleaner's and the post office, because Mrs Flittersnoop always thought she ought to do as much as possible when she came out shopping, as it seemed a pity not to.

'I'd better, um, ah, go back and see where I left it,' said the Professor.

'Oh no, indeed, I'm not sure, sir!' cried Mrs Flittersnoop. 'Can't you remember which shop you left it in?'

'If I could remember which shop I left it in, I shouldn't um, ah, have left it there,' said the Professor. 'I'll start with the last shop we went to.'

But he found he couldn't remember which shop that was. Mrs Flittersnoop was just going to remind him, when up came Colonel Dedshott of the Catapult Cavaliers with his medals jingling.

'Ha, morning, my word, what!' he said. 'Thought it was going to rain but it's stopped, by Jove!'

Mrs Flittersnoop saw the opportunity of a convenient rescue from the umbrella situation and asked the Colonel if he'd help her find the Professor's lost umbrella.

'Ha, my word, yes!' said the Colonel. 'You give me a list of the shops you've been to and I'll get my Catapult Cavaliers to search.'

But while Mrs Flittersnoop was giving him the list of shops, who should come rushing up but Miss Frenzie of the Pagwell Publishing Company, closely followed by Violet, each on her own skateboard, as Violet had refused to travel on the same one as Miss Frenzie.

'Don't you worry, my dear man,' said Miss Frenzie, running into a lamp-post, which was the only way she could be sure of stopping her skateboard without falling off it. 'We'll pop round the shops and find the lost umbrella. Come on, Violet!' And off she shot, followed by Violet.

'But they don't know which shops we've been to,' said Mrs

Flittersnoop, gathering up shopping bags and dropping parcels.

But that didn't worry Miss Frenzie. She was already making a frantic round of every shop in the town.

Then Colonel Dedshott set off to organize a Catapult Cavalier search for the missing umbrella just in time to miss Commander Hardaport (Retired), who came steaming round the opposite corner with all sails set.

'What's that? Umbrella lost overboard!' he said, when the Professor explained what had happened. 'Soon find it for you. Cruise round the shops. Bound to find it.' He turned and tacked off zigzag between the traffic and ran into the Vicar on the other side of the road. 'Professor Branestawm left umbrella in shop!' he shouted. 'Off to find it!'

'Dear me,' said the Vicar, making sure he had his own umbrella, which he always carried night and day in case somebody's prayers for rain got answered. He carefully crossed at the traffic lights when it was safe and began helping Mrs Flittersnoop and the Professor collect their parcels.

Meantime Commander Hardaport (Retired) had met the Vicar's twin daughters, Maisie and Daisie, out shopping for something different in the way of identical outfits. He told them about the Professor's lost umbrella and they set off as well to help find it. And on the way they encountered Lord Pagwell. He thought it would be easier to buy a new umbrella rather than spend time looking for one you'd lost, when you didn't know where you'd lost it. But he agreed to help Maisie and Daisie in the search.

'Now you go to the post office, Professor, and see if you left the umbrella there, while I go back to the cleaner's,' said Mrs Flittersnoop, getting all organized.

'Pray, allow me to take your shopping home,' said the Vicar, who thought that would be easier than looking for lost-goodness-knows-where umbrellas, but, in fact, it was a lot more difficult as there was enough shopping to overload three vicars. Fortunately a heap of scouts and girl guides arrived with a little cart and took all the shopping back to the Professor's house, while the Professor and Mrs Flittersnoop set off to look for the lost umbrella and the Vicar went into the nearest church to say a prayer to St Anthony, who looks after lost property.

The Professor eventually arrived at the post office, but not before he'd seen a notice on a shop saying 'Umbrellas Recovered', and it took an awful lot of explaining talk on both sides before he discovered that the people in the shop didn't find lost umbrellas, but put new covers on not-lost old ones.

So by the time he got to the post office he felt even more lost than his umbrella.

'Now, where do I, um, ah, enquire about lost umbrellas?' he asked himself. There were queues of people at various counters, some of which were marked 'Stamps', some 'Postal Orders', some 'Savings Bank', some 'Parcels', and some without any queues at them, but they were marked 'Closed'.

'Dear me,' said the Professor. 'I shall never find my umbrella here with all these people.' But just then he saw an umbrella hooked over a counter where people could write letters, if they could do it with a dried-up ball-pen fastened to a little chain in case it got stolen.

'Ha, there it is!' he cried and, picking up the umbrella, he went home.

But oh, good gracious, and whatever! It wasn't the Professor's umbrella at all. It belonged to a gentleman who had started to write a postcard to his granddaughter in Western Australia, found he didn't have the right stamps for it, and who'd gone to join the stamp queue, leaving his umbrella at the writing desk.

Meantime Commander Hardaport (Retired) had discovered the Professor's umbrella at Ginnibag & Knitwoddle's, which was fairly easy because they had a special room right at the top of the building where all lost property that had been found was sent. And there was the Professor's umbrella keeping company with shopping bags, odd gloves, walking sticks, forgotten scarves, overlooked spectacles and all the other things that people leave in shops.

Colonel Dedshott went striding into a supermarket to ask if the Professor had left his umbrella there. And he had.

'We put it aside until he came back for it, sir,' said the manager, who knew Colonel Dedshott, 'so perhaps you'd take it and return it to him.' Which the Colonel did, after filling up seven forms in triplicate, guaranteeing to absolve the supermarket from any claims made by the Professor or his heirs or assigns in connection with the said umbrella.

Then Miss Frenzie found another of the Professor's umbrellas at the ironmonger's, and Violet unearthed one at the Garden Centre, where he'd left it hooked over the arm of a stone nymph, who looked as if she needed something more than an umbrella to cover her up, whether it rained or not.

Of course all these umbrellas *did* belong to the Professor, because he often left his umbrella in a shop, and took another one with him the next time he went out. He could do this as he had several umbrellas, some of which were special ones of his own invention.

It was one of these specially invented umbrellas that a dear old lady collected from The Needlework Corner where she'd left her own umbrella. One of the Catapult Cavaliers had taken hers by mistake, thinking it was the Professor's.

Then Maisie and Daisie each found another umbrella in different shops, but neither of these belonged to the Professor either. The shop people hadn't noticed who had left the umbrellas, and when they were asked by Maisie and Daisie if the Professor had left his umbrella there, they assumed that he had, since he often went into their shops and frequently left things behind.

'Oh my goodness, indeed, I never!' cried Mrs Flittersnoop, who'd given up looking for the Professor's umbrella and gone home, as strange umbrellas began arriving every hour. 'I know the Professor had several umbrellas, but I'm sure he never had as many as this.'

Then the news got round not only that Professor Branestawm had left his umbrella in a shop somewhere, but that he'd left all sorts of other things, which he actually hadn't, though he certainly might have done.

So more and more umbrellas began to come in, closely followed by walking sticks, hockey sticks and shooting sticks, which the people in various shops had found and thought Professor Branestawm must have left behind. But really other people had, because Professor Branestawm wasn't the only absent-minded person in Pagwell, though he could do it rather better than others.

'I shall, um, er, have to go out and leave these things in other shops,' said the Professor, 'so as to, er, get rid of them.'

'That won't be any good, sir!' cried Mrs Flittersnoop. 'The people will only send them back again!'

Out in the wilds of Pagwell High Street, in the middle of a shower of rain, the old lady who'd got the Professor's patent umbrella by mistake for her own opened it. Showers of nuts and bolts and screws and hammers and wire cutters and other inventing machinery fell out *bing, splang, rattle, ding, ding* all over the pavement.

People rushed up to help collect the things, and wondered what an old lady was doing with all that stuff.

Then a policeman appeared on the scene.

'Here, there now, then, I say,' he said. 'That's Professor

Branestawm's umbrella. I recognize it because he demonstrated it at the police station. How do you account for it being in your possession, madam?' he asked the old lady.

But the old lady was so astonished at what had happened, on top of which she had no idea how she came to have the Professor's umbrella, besides which she didn't know it was the Professor's umbrella, that she couldn't say anything.

Fortunately the Vicar was just coming out of a nearby church and grasped the situation, explained matters to the policeman and took the old lady into Ye Old Bunne Shoppe for a soothing cup of tea.

The manageress of Ye Olde Bunne Shoppe was delighted to see him.

'Oh, Vicar!' she cried. 'You're just the man I want to see. Professor Branestawm left his umbrella here and I was hoping he'd come back in for it, but you'll do.' And she gave the Vicar yet another umbrella.

But the old lady said, 'Why, that's my umbrella. What was Professor Branestawm doing with my umbrella? Hasn't he got enough umbrellas of his own to leave in shops? I left that umbrella in The Needlework Corner, but they said they hadn't got it when I went back for it.'

'Evidently the Professor took it in mistake for his own,' said the Vicar, but, of course, it was actually one of the Catapult Cavaliers who had taken it from The Needlework Corner and left it in the tea-shop by mistake.

'Well,' said the old lady, finishing her third soothing cup of tea and snatching the umbrella, 'it's a nice thing, I must say, if a person can't leave her umbrella in a shop without professors taking it and leaving it in other shops. I don't know what the country's coming to. It's all this inflation and VAT and balance of payments we hear so much about, that's what it is. I knew no good would come of it. We were better off with pounds, shillings and pence, and gas lamps in the streets.' And she stumped off to catch a bus home.

But by this time there was a queue and a half outside the Professor's house, with people bringing umbrellas and walking sticks and shopping bags and parcels and bird cages and electric waffle irons and out-of-order alarm clocks, which people had left in various places and which other people thought belonged to the Professor.

'Dear me, this is, um, ah, awful!' gasped the Professor, waving his arms, and some of the people in the queue waved back either to be friendly or to try to hurry things up as they didn't want to wait. It's a strange thing that people say they never want to wait in queues, yet they join queues for the express purpose of waiting. Professors aren't the only rummy people.

'However can we get rid of all these people and all these things?' wailed Mrs Flittersnoop, as the dining-room, the hall and the kitchen became fuller and fuller of things that didn't belong to them and they wouldn't have wanted if they had.

Pagwell Gazette sent round their best reporter, who started asking people in the queue questions and got enough material to fill the paper for the next ten editions, which would have squeezed out the weddings if the editor had let it.

Colonel Dedshott was all for calling out the Catapult Cavaliers and marching everyone off to a surplus disposal camp, which is what the Army does with things they have no further use for.

Commander Hardaport (Retired) went home and locked himself in his little cabin study because, being a sailor and very tidy by nature, he couldn't stand the sight of so many people and things littering the place up.

Miss Frenzie started planning a special Friends-of-Lost-Property Club to go round collecting things people had left behind and returning them to their rightful owners.

Professor Branestawm was in a terrible state.

'I'd try to invent a machine for getting rid of unwanted lost property,' he said, 'only with all these, um, ah, people about I can't get into my, ah, inventory.'

Then, like an appropriate gift from Heaven, came the Vicar of Pagwell accompanied by the Bishop, three acolytes and no end of scouts and girl guides with the same little trucks that had proved so useful in moving the Ancient Roman remains from the vicarage garden.

'Ha, my dear Professor!' cried the Vicar. 'Pray let us be of assistance.'

Then, while the Bishop said some special prayers, assisted by the acolytes whenever he forgot the words, the Vicar organized a gigantic bring-and-take-away-sale-or-exchange at the church hall. Everybody brought everything they thought the Professor had left in shops or other places, and the Professor and Mrs Flittersnoop brought all the lost property that had been returned to them even though they hadn't left it in shops and other places.

And a pleasant day was spent by one and all when, to the accompaniment of home-made cakes and instant tea, everyone got back his own property if he or she wanted it, or sold it if he or she didn't, to someone who did. And the church funds were donated a small commission on these transactions, so everyone was satisfied.

7
Rainbow Roads

In Pagwell High Street a gentleman in a bright orange jacket was painting a bright yellow line along by the kerb. Yellow lines, as everybody knows, keep motor cars away, just as yellow lamps keep mosquitoes away, red flannel keeps colds away, and apples a day keep doctors away. But unfortunately yellow lines don't keep ladies with little trolleys full of shopping away, and one of them ran wallop into Professor Branestawm, who had just been run into by a new world-shaking idea. And the world-shaking idea had been brought on by the yellow line, so yellow lines don't keep world-shaking ideas away either, so what use are they?

'Oh, I'm so sorry!' said the lady, picking up cut-price groceries with one hand and apologizing with the other.

'Not at, er, um, at all,' said the Professor. He raised his hat and out of it fell a packet of special no-cook, no-stir, no-trouble, ready-mixed pancake composition he'd bought for Mrs Flittersnoop. The trolley lady swept it up thinking it was hers and wondered when she got home what she wanted it for.

'All these yellow lines really do not make the roads any safer,' mumbled the Professor to himself. 'In fact, there really seems more danger from pedestrians than from vehicles.' He just avoided being knocked down by a double-decker pram, dodged a folding push-cart containing an unfolding and rather rowdy baby, and collided with an old gentleman in a cap carrying two bags full of goodness knows what. But he got home safely with the idea the yellow lines had given him.

'People', he said to Mrs Flittersnoop, 'are always losing their way.'

'Yes, indeed, I'm sure, sir,' she said, saying nothing about the Professor losing her special self-operating pancake composition, because she didn't want to start anything complicated.

'All these yellow lines in the roads don't help,' went on the Professor, 'but they could if they were different colours.'

Mrs Flittersnoop wondered how yellow lines that were a different colour could stop people losing their way, but the Professor soon un-wondered her.

'My idea is', he said, starting to wave his spectacles about, 'to have the roads painted with lines of different colours to show the way to places.'

'I'll just put the kettle on,' said Mrs Flittersnoop, who reckoned she'd be able to do with a nice cup of tea before long if the Professor was off on an explaining talk.

'If you wanted to go to the library, for instance,' he said, 'you would simply follow the blue line. To get to the park the green line would guide you. A red line for the fire station and so on. I'm glad you're surprised,' he said, 'but you need not, um, ah, whistle so loudly.'

But it wasn't Mrs Flittersnoop whistling, it was the kettle saying it was time to make the tea.

'Very clever, I'm sure, sir,' said Mrs Flittersnoop, operating cups and saucers, 'but suppose people went the wrong way. I mean to say, sir, if I may make so bold, if the blue line led to the library in one direction, if one followed it the opposite way, it would lead away from the library, wouldn't it?'

'No, no, no, no, you don't understand!' cried the Professor, stirring his tea with a pair of spectacles. 'One cannot go the wrong way. The traffic laws don't, er, um, allow it. You have to keep to the left and, wherever you happened to be, the blue line leading to the, ah, library would be on the left side of the road and you'd have to go the right way. On the other hand, if it was a one-way street you could only go one way. With my idea it will be impossible to go the wrong way along a two-way street.

Mrs Flittersnoop thought it was a bit difficult to do that as i was, but she got out the coconut finger biscuits and said nothing

Professor Branestawm for once didn't have much troubl persuading the Pagwell Council to adopt his idea, though on councillor said it would make the place look like a crazy game o snakes and ladders. Another councillor said it would send peopl round the bend, to which Professor Branestawm replied that a least it would send them round the right bend to get where the wanted to be.

The only councillor who really objected was a lady who sai she couldn't stop to argue as she had to go and queue for bananas of which there was a sudden shortage.

'Um, ah, very well, gentlemen,' said the Professor, arrangin his spectacles in the right order and feeling very pleased wit himself and everybody else, 'we can now proceed wit painting the, um, ah, roads in the required colours.'

'Here, hold hard a moment,' said the Town Clerk, who fel there ought to be a bye-law against things being so easy. 'W haven't decided what colour will be used to show the way to eac of the town's amenities.'

'Well,' said the Professor, 'that should be quite, um, simple For instance, take the library. What would be a suitable colou for that?'

'I reckon it should be red because books are read,' said councillor, who thought he should be funny as it was a nice day

'Wait a minute!' protested the Chief Postman. 'Red's a Pos Office colour, you know. Post Office vans are red and come t that letters are read, too, if we're going to be all that comic.'

'What about the fire station?' cried the Chief Fireman, wh was very quick on things as he was used to dashing off to fires 'Red's a fire station colour, red fire engines, red flames and so on

'But,' said the Professor, waving his hands, 'nobody wants to go to the fire station except the firemen and they already know the way. It's the fire station that has to go to other people so to, er, um, ah, speak.'

'Oh, all right,' grumbled the Chief Fireman, making up his mind not to hurry too much if the Professor's house caught fire, 'but I think it's rather insulting to the fire service for people not to know the way to it.'

There was a bit of mixed-up argument between the Chief Postman and the Head Librarian about who should have red for his colour, but eventually the Librarian said he'd agree to red being used for the post office and they'd have blue for the library.

'Now then, now then!' cried the Chief Policeman, trying to put his thumbs into his belt, but finding it difficult as he wasn't wearing one. 'We can't have that you know. Everybody knows blue is the police station colour. Blue lamp, boys in blue and all that.'

'Well I don't know about that, sir,' said a police sergeant, who had come along to support the Chief Policeman. 'I don't know that people want to know where the police station is all that much.' He was a bit bothered with dear old ladies coming in about their lost doggies. 'I reckon the people who most need to go to the police station are those who commit crimes, and we'll be only too pleased to show them the way without any coloured lines on the roads.'

'Well, anyway, blue is the right colour for the library,' said the Head Librarian. 'It's a very educational colour. That's why very cultured and highly intellectual ladies are called blue stockings.'

'They don't wear 'em any more,' said a councillor, whose wife kept a ladies' dress shop. 'It's all tights nowadays, and I don't think highly educated ladies would care to be called blue tights.'

'I fail to see how the question of whether educated ladies wear blue stockings or blue tights has anything to, um, ah, do with the

colour of roads,' said the Professor in a very frosty voice tha
made the Mayor's morning tea go cold.

So blue was agreed for the library, and the Parks and Garden
Councillor voted for green for the park and nobody coul
disagree with that, although some of them might have liked t
because it would have made them feel important.

'Then there's the hospital,' said Doctor Mumpzanmeazle. '
think we should have yellow for that.'

'People will confuse that with the yellow lines that mean N
Parking,' said the Traffic Councillor.

'Make it yellow with red spots,' said the funny councillor.

At last it was decided that stripes should be painted on al
roads, in colours according to where the roads led, that is to say
viz., and as follows:

Red for roads leading to the post office.

Blue for the library.

Green for the parks.

Pink for the hospital, because that was the colour the hospita
people hoped you'd be when you came out.

Purple for Pagwell Cathedral and the churches, because tha
was a nice devotional church colour.

'Ah now, there is a point here,' said a councillor, jabbing hi
pencil on the table and accidentally spearing the Town Clerk'
morning doughnut. 'There are several churches in Pagwell, s
how do people know that the purple line will take them to the on
they want?'

'I had, er, um, thought of that,' said the Professor, who ha
actually only thought of it that second. 'The same thing of cours
applies to cinemas of which there are, um, ah, several. The sam
coloured stripe will lead to them all, but with arrows pointing o
at each church or, ah, cinema, as required.'

Dotted red and green lines were agreed for the theatres an
cinemas, because they often had dotty plays on.

The Mayor wanted special lines in fluorescent paint to lead to his house so that he could find his way home at night, but that was ruled out of order.

And finally they had a nice milk-chocolate brown for the railway station, because the initials of British Rail looked like a short version of brown, and also because people sometimes got very slightly browned off if a train was late, or the windows of the trains, by some oversight, hadn't been cleaned.

'This is all very well,' said a councillor, who hadn't said anything yet because he had his mouth full of morning bun, 'but how are visitors to the town going to know what coloured stripes in the roads are for? And even if they know that, how are they to know that the red stripe leads to the post office, and so on?'

'We shall erect notices at the boundaries of Pagwell,' said the Professor. 'Some places I believe already have, er, um, notices saying "Welcome to Whereveritis" and some even tell you to drive carefully, as if they thought their town was dangerous.' He stuffed his spectacles in his pocket, drank the Town Clerk's tea and went on. 'There will be a notice board as you enter Pagwell, saying "How to find your way in Pagwell—follow the coloured stripe." Then there will be a colour code saying where each colour leads. Nothing could be simpler.'

'Yes, it could,' said a councillor, who liked to argue. 'Nothing at all would be a lot simpler.'

'Pah,' snorted the Professor and they all went home, except the Professor, who went round to the Municipal Road-Painting Department and had a lot of words with the Head Painter of White Lines about painting coloured ones.

'We don't have no coloured paint for painting lines on roads, sir,' said the Head Painter.

'Tut, tut,' said the Professor, 'we don't want no-coloured paint, we want coloured paint.'

'Yes, sir,' said the man, tipping his cap to the back of his head to help him think, which it didn't do much. 'That's what I mean, sir, we don't have no paint what's coloured, so to speak. It's all white.'

'It's not all white at all, it's all wong, er, um, I mean wrong,' said the Professor, getting all confused. 'We must get some coloured paint.'

'Paint for road do be special sort of paint, sir,' said the Head Painter. 'So's the rain don't wash it off, nor the motor car wheels rub it off like. And they don't make that sort of paint in all them colours, they don't, sir.'

'Oh, all right,' said the Professor. 'I shall just have to invent some coloured paint for roads, that's all.' And he went home to his inventory to do just that.

The day of the Rainbow Roads dawned over Pagwell bright and early with the sky doing its best to show it had more colour than the Pagwell streets, but it was a bit sneaky about saying where the various coloured stripes led, so they weren't much help to the jumbo jets.

The Mayor of Pagwell ceremoniously cut a rainbow coloured ribbon to open the scheme, and various important personages set out for the first ride on the coloured roads.

The Mayor arrived safely at the library and was presented with a specially bound volume of the bye-laws, one of which said no colours but red, green and amber were to be used for traffic signs, and none of which said roads could be painted in coloured stripes.

The Vicar of Pagwell accompanied by the Bishop managed to pop in at five different churches and the cathedral, where they received a cup of weak tea and a hot cross bun, although it wasn't Easter.

The Chief Postman reached the post office just in time to miss the post, but in time to be given a framed set of used stamps

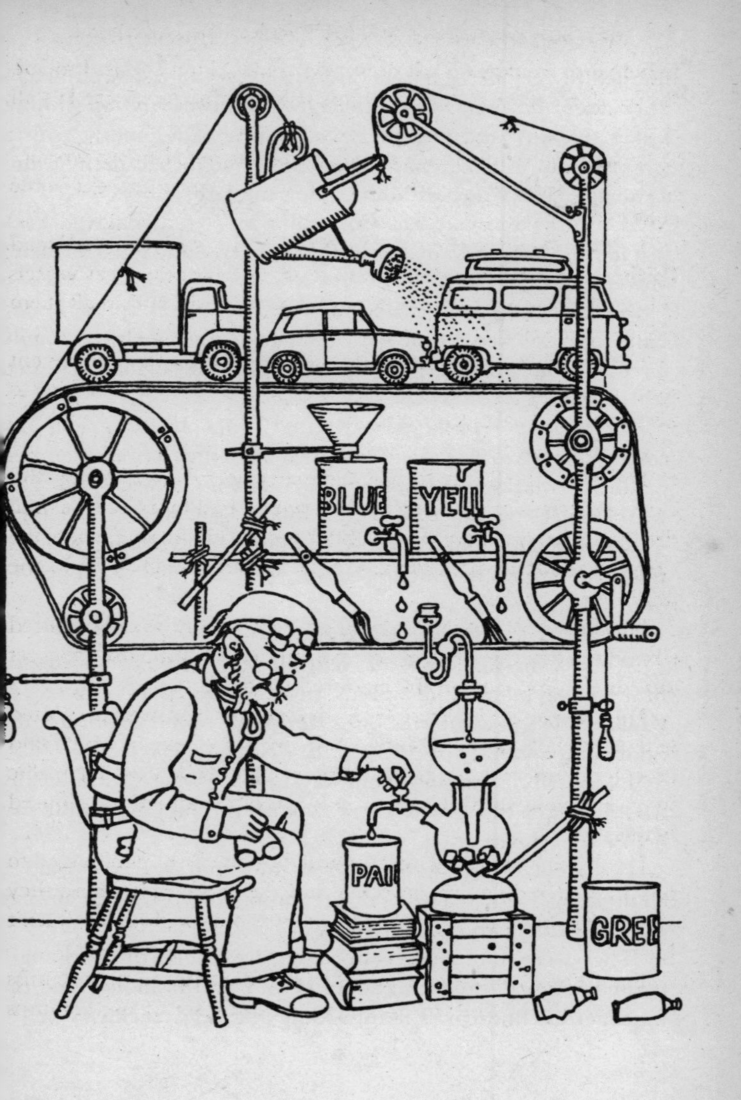
BLUE
YELL
PAI
GREE

marked in very fierce letters 'insufficient postage, ten p to pay'.

Professor Branestawm got to Pagwell Railway Station without losing the way and was presented very ceremoniously with a season platform ticket that permitted him to miss as many trains as he liked every day without paying the fare.

The Parks and Gardens Councillor arrived at Pagwell Park just in time to help Lady Pagwell plant a tree and got a spadeful of wet soil in his boots.

Doctor Mumpzanmeazle reached Pagwell Hospital at the same time as three people with stomach ache, which was handy for them, but awkward for him, as he missed being presented with a special stethoscope.

Commander Hardaport (Retired), not being given any coloured roads to ride along, stamped off to the river and shouted nautical remarks at the boats, which took no notice.

Colonel Dedshott with a detachment of Catapult Cavaliers trotted jinglingly along the roads, not minding very much which coloured stripes they followed, as long as they got back to barracks in time for lunch.

'Well I, um, ah, think all went off very well,' said Professor Branestawm later, as he and his friends gathered at Ginnibag & Knitwoddle's restaurant for a little party to celebrate the rainbow roads.

'Everybody is finding their way to everywhere without any trouble,' said the Town Clerk, taking the last doughnut just before the Mayor got it.

'It should do a lot of good to our tourist trade,' said a councillor. 'I noticed several foreign-looking people in strange clothes walking about the streets.'

'They were some models from our dress department doing a mannequin walk-about to advertise our new fashions,' said the manager of Ginnibag & Knitwoddle in a very crackly voice.

But whether or not the rainbow roads did any good to Pagwell's tourist trade, they certainly did a lot of good to people in the various outer Pagwells, who, when they came into Great Pagwell, were delighted to be able to find their way about for once. It also did a certain amount of good in the post office where the queues for stamps grew twice the length now people could find their way there, and to British Rail, whose trains became stuffed with travellers, who had never been able to find the railway station before and who consequently had had to go everywhere by bus, changing five times. And the library was discovered by so many readers they had to buy absolute mountains more books and would have had to buy miles more shelves, only the books went out so quickly they didn't need them.

'I cannot, um, er, ah, understand it,' said Professor Branestawm through his spectacles, which had slipped down over his mouth.

'Astounding, my word, what!' cried Colonel Dedshott, shooting his eyebrows up and down in surprise.

'Lot of landlubbers,' barked Commander Hardaport (Retired), puffing like a second-hand paddle-steamer.

'It really is most extraordinary,' murmured the Vicar.

'I knew no good would come of it,' said the Town Clerk, who always felt the one compensation for things going wrong was having something to complain about.

For Professor Branestawm's brilliant rainbow roads had gone mad. Or at least they'd done a sort of conjuring trick and changed colour without asking the Council's permission first.

Chaos not only reigned, it had jubilee celebrations. People were trying to take books out at the railway station, going to the hospitals for sevenpenny stamps, and expecting to be cured of spots, coughs, colds and ingrowing eyelashes at the library.

An Oriental gentleman in a tremendous motor car, which had everything except a bathroom, lost his way to the bank, and the bank had to send bagsful of lovely money out to him accompanied by security guards, scouts and district nurses.

But this time it was no one person's fault that a Branestawm invention had resulted in assorted disasters. If the Vicar hadn't prayed for rain and got an answer in the form of a heavy thunderstorm accompanied by hail. If the sun hadn't come out next morning and scorched the place up. If the Pagwell Council paint man hadn't got the wrong paint through getting his forms muddled in triplicate. And if a tankful of bad-tempered chemical from the Combined Pagwells Chemical Corporation hadn't got spilt on the roads, everything might have been all right. But all these things combined, plus a few others, caused the coloured stripes in the roads to fade and get mixed together and change colour. So Pagwell Council just had to have all the roads painted a nice quiet street grey and leave people to find their own way about as before.

But by now most people had found their way to the variou places, partly through following the coloured lines in the first instance, and partly by following the altered ones later and finding they'd got to the wrong places.

'After all,' they said, 'you can't have everything, and even i you did it would probably be too much.'

So Professor Branestawm's idea wasn't wasted after all because Pagwell Council painted coloured stripes in the children's playground to make a sort of rainbow maze, which wa nice and safe because if you got drastically lost, you could jus walk across the coloured lines and go home.

Professor Branestawm finished up at the railway station, where he tried to take out a book of stamps, but they gave him a cup o British Rail coffee instead, which set him off thinking about an invention to make coffee that tasted as good as it smelt.

8

A Date with Miss Frenzie

Professor Branestawm's telephone went *brrring brrring, brrring brrring.* It was an ordinary telephone and not one of the Professor's inventions, because the telephone people don't take kindly to people having funny telephones.

'Hullo,' said Mrs Flittersnoop, picking up the receiver.

'Miss Frenzie of the Pagwell Publishing Company would like to speak to Professor Branestawm,' said a voice. It was Miss Frenzie's secretary, Violet.

'Yes, indeed, I'm sure,' said Mrs Flittersnoop. 'Put Miss Frenzie on, and I'll go and fetch the Professor.'

'Oh, I'm afraid I can't do that,' said Violet. 'Miss Frenzie is much too busy to be kept waiting. You go and get the Professor and then I'll put Miss Frenzie on.'

Mrs Flittersnoop drew herself up to her Sunday-best height and said in a very well-bred voice:

'I'm very sorry, I'm sure, but the Professor is busy too. He is in his inventory and does not like being disturbed. But since it is Miss Frenzie,' she added, 'I will fetch him, if you put Miss Frenzie on.'

'No good, I'm afraid,' said Violet. 'Miss Frenzie won't answer the phone until the Professor is on the other end.'

'Then', said Mrs Flittersnoop, 'I do not really see why the Professor should answer the phone until Miss Frenzie is on the other end, if I may say so.'

'Oh dear,' said Violet. 'Then if neither of them will come on till the other one does, there's nothing we can do about it, is there?'

'No, indeed, I'm sure,' said Mrs Flittersnoop. They both rang off, and the telephone people got tuppence, or whatever it is, without anybody else getting anything for it.

'Oh, but I'd have come to the phone for Miss Frenzie,' said the Professor, when Mrs Flittersnoop told him about it. 'I know she's always very busy.'

'I didn't consider it proper', said Mrs Flittersnoop, folding her arms indignantly, 'that you should be kept waiting for anyone. Unless, of course, it was the Queen,' she added. But Professor Branestawm didn't think it very likely the Queen would ring him up. They have enough problems at Buckingham Palace without getting Professor Branestawm involved.

'Well, I don't know what Miss Frenzie wanted to speak to me about,' said the Professor, 'but as it seems to be, um, ah, impossible to speak to her on the phone, I had better write and invite her to come over.'

So he wrote a letter to Miss Frenzie asking if she would care to come over for a cup of tea the following Thursday morning.

In the meantime Miss Frenzie was telling Violet she wouldn't have minded hanging on the phone for Professor Branestawm, but in the circumstances she thought she'd better write and ask him to come and see her. So she did, and made the invitation for next Thursday morning too. Things like that can happen in Pagwell.

Next Thursday arrived dead on time and Professor Branestawm sat in his sitting-room, with Mrs Flittersnoop all ready to hover with the tea things when Miss Frenzie arrived.

'You don't think you should have gone to see her, do you, sir?' Mrs Flittersnoop asked. 'I mean to say she did write and ask you for today.'

'I know she did,' said the Professor, 'but I had already written to ask her to come here, so I will wait for her.'

But after an hour or so the Professor began to have doubts.

'Perhaps she didn't get my letter,' he said, 'or she may be thinking I am going to see her, as she invited me.'

Over at the Pagwell Publishing Company Miss Frenzie, surrounded by Violet, was saying, 'I suppose the Professor has forgotten all about our appointment, he is so absent-minded.'

'Perhaps he expects you to go and see him, as he invited you,' said Violet, messing about with her typewriter, which let out pinging noises.

'Well it's no use ringing him up or we shall have that same silly business of neither of us talking to the other,' said Miss Frenzie. 'I'd better go over and see him.'

So off she set in a rather prehistoric motor car, but when she arrived at the Professor's house he wasn't there.

'He left only a little while back to visit you,' said Mrs Flittersnoop. '*As you asked him to*,' she added, feeling a bit peeved that the tea had gone stewed and her hot scones cold.

'Oh dear!' cried Miss Frenzie, tearing out some hair, which didn't help and only made her hat go crooked. 'I'd better go back. If he should come home, having missed me at my place, tell him to stay here and I'll come back.'

Before Mrs Flittersnoop had time to say, 'Yes, indeed, I'm sure,' Miss Frenzie burst off and arrived back at the Pagwell Publishing Company, only to find the Professor had been and gone again.

'I told him you'd gone to see him as he asked you,' said Violet, beginning to wish she was in the Army or somewhere else nice and quiet. 'He left a message that I was to keep you here if you came back and he'll come back here to see you.'

Oh, frightful situation! Here was Miss Frenzie stuck in her office waiting for Professor Branestawm to come back and there was Professor Branestawm at home waiting for Miss Frenzie to come over.

Lunch-time came and went. Miss Frenzie ate Violet's sandwiches, so as not to be out if the Professor came. Professor Branestawm didn't like to have lunch in case Miss Frenzie arrived in the middle of it, and Mrs Flittersnoop didn't know what to do, she was sure.

'Oh, I can't wait all day for the man!' said Miss Frenzie at last, when Violet's sandwiches were finished. 'I'm going over to see him!' and off she shot.

But on the way her motor car passed a Pagwell taxi with Professor Branestawm in it, on his way to see her, his own car being in bits for improvement.

'She's only just left. If you dash back you'll catch her at your place,' cried Violet, when the Professor arrived.

'The Professor's only been gone a few moments. If you go back at once, you'll be there as soon as he is,' said Mrs Flittersnoop, when Miss Frenzie arrived.

Zim, zim, zim, pouff, bang, rattle, tick, tock. Miss Frenzie and Professor Branestawm shot through the streets of Pagwell and passed each other again as they went back to their own places once more.

'This is ridiculous!' exclaimed Miss Frenzie. 'We will never meet at this rate. We must get the thing properly organized. Now, Violet,' she said, 'you get on your motor bike, go to Professor Branestawm's house and keep him there till I arrive.'

'Righto,' said Violet and, pausing only to cover her typewriter, put a bar of chocolate in her handbag, comb her hair, do her eyebrows, touch up her eye make-up, and put on a yellow safety driving coat and a crash helmet that made her look like something from outermost space, she shot off.

But the Professor was also bending his mind to the problem of not missing Miss Frenzie.

'This, um, ah, calls for some organization,' he said. 'I'd be greatly, um, ah, obliged Mrs Flittersnoop if you'd cycle over to

Miss Frenzie's for me while I sort some things out here. Tell her to wait there. Don't let her start for here whatever you do. Keep her in her office and I will come on and meet her there as soon as I can.'

Mrs Flittersnoop said nothing, but cycled carefully and with proper dignity off to Miss Frenzie's.

Of course she and Violet might have met on the way and managed to sort things out between them. But Violet took the route through Great Pagwell High Street because she wanted to buy some new and exotic eye shadow and so got delayed on the way; while Mrs Flittersnoop went by the side roads, so as to avoid the traffic, which always made her nervous when she was cycling.

Miss Frenzie still hadn't left when Mrs Flittersnoop arrived, because she'd come across some frightfully urgent papers that had to be dealt with at once.

'Oh well,' she said, when Mrs Flittersnoop arrived with the message, 'I sent Violet to keep him there, but if he's coming over in any case, I'll wait for him.'

But the Professor had got caught up with a bit of spare inventing and hadn't set off at once for Miss Frenzie's, so he was still there when Violet arrived. And, of course, when Violet told the Professor to wait where he was because Miss Frenzie was on her way over, what could he do? One can't refuse a polite request from a nice girl with exotic eye shadow, can one? Certainly the Professor couldn't, not so much because he was hypnotized by Violet's eye shadow, as because he never knew what to say to girls. So he sat down to wait for Miss Frenzie, while she was sitting down in her office to wait for him.

While they were waiting Mrs Flittersnoop offered to make Miss Frenzie a cup of tea, but the Pagwell Publishing Company was too modern to have teapots and things like that. They had an enormous sort of tank with square eyes and little levers that gave you tea or coffee, whichever you didn't want, in a little paper cup that you had to shove under the spout instantly or the tea/coffee went all over your feet. And if you did manage to catch it in the cup, the cup immediately became too hot and you dropped it and the tea/coffee on your feet anyway.

While Mrs Flittersnoop was operating the machine on instructions from Miss Frenzie and getting cups of boiling water and showers of instant coffee all over the floor, Violet, back at the Professor's, was offering to type some letters for him.

'This is, um, ah, very kind of you,' murmured the Professor, 'but I have no letters to write at the moment. Unless I write to Miss Frenzie asking her to come over, but then, since you say she is already on the way, that would be rather, um, ah, unnecessary.'

Oh, quite,' said Violet. But she put a sheet of paper into Professor Branestawm's typewriter in case. And rather wished she hadn't because it typed a not very polite message intended for the Pagwell Council that nearly made her eye shadow go all runny.

'We can't wait about here all day for the Professor,' said Miss Frenzie to Mrs Flittersnoop. 'Violet must have got to him with my message to wait for me after he sent you to tell me to wait for him, so he probably doesn't know what to do. We'd better both go over to him.'

But at that moment Professor Branestawm was rescuing Violet from his typewriter and they both set off on Violet's motor bike for the Pagwell Publishing Company.

And, as they took different routes, they missed each other again.

Now Professor Branestawm and Violet were at the Pagwell Publishing Company, which was just going to close, and Miss Frenzie and Mrs Flittersnoop were at the Professor's.

'I'm not waiting any longer,' said Miss Frenzie. 'I've got to

give a talk at the Pagwell Institute for Distracted Authors, so I'll be off. When the Professor comes in, tell him I'm sorry I missed him.'

'Yes, indeed, I'm sure,' said Mrs Flittersnoop and sank into an armchair.

'I'm afraid I shall have to go now,' said Violet to the Professor. 'The office is closing, so you'll have to go too. Can I call you a taxi?'

'I have been, um, ah, called more impolite things,' said the Professor, 'but no, no, my dear, I'll just walk along to the library. Perhaps Miss Frenzie will, um, ah, write and tell me what it was she wished to see me about.'

'Ha, ha, yes, rather,' said Violet, reckoning Miss Frenzie might have done that in the first place, only it was rather too simple.

So the Professor set off for the library, got muddled, forgot where he was going and arrived at the Institute for Distracted Authors just in time to miss Miss Frenzie's talk.

But at last they met, even if it was where neither of them had intended. Only Miss Frenzie had had so many things to think about all at once, she thought it was the Professor who had wanted to see her. And the Professor had forgotten that it was Miss Frenzie who wanted to see him and not the other way round. So neither of them could think of what it was either of them wanted to see the other about.

But all that rushing about missing each other wasn't one hundred per cent wasted because the Professor was able to meet several authors who gave him absorbing descriptions of how good their books were. The Professor thought he might invent a machine for writing books, but then decided it would be too dangerous.

9
The Big Zipper

'I, um, ah, believe it is your birthday today, Mrs Flittersnoop,' said the Professor one breakfast-time.

'Yes, indeed, I'm sure, sir,' smiled Mrs Flittersnoop, who had entered a little note in the Professor's diary to remind him of that interesting fact. Of course, the Professor would probably have forgotten to look in his diary, only Mrs Flittersnoop had put it under his plate to make sure.

'I, um, ah, think this calls for a little, um, celebration,' said the Professor. 'Would you care to meet me for tea this afternoon at Ginnibag & Knitwoddle's restaurant?'

Mrs Flittersnoop said she'd be delighted.

'I've got a little shopping to do, sir, if that's all right with you, so I'll meet you in the restaurant. Shall we say half past four?'

So the Professor said 'half past four'. Mrs Flittersnoop cleared away the breakfast things and went into the kitchen, while the Professor went into his inventory.

Strangely enough, Professor Branestawm remembered about taking Mrs Flittersnoop to tea.

'Ginnibag & Knitwoddle's at half past four,' he said and off he went. When he got to Ginnibag & Knitwoddle there was a notice on the double doors at the front saying 'Please use other door.' It meant, of course, that you were to use the right-hand door and not the left-hand one, because that one was being mended and wouldn't open.

But Professor Branestawm, always ready to obey polite requests, thought it meant 'Don't use this entrance', and he went round the back of the building to the other entrance to the store.

But the double doors at that entrance also had one door out of action and a notice saying 'Please use other door.'

'Dear me,' said the Professor. 'It seems one cannot get into the store although it's open; though I fail to see how a store can be open, if you cannot use the doors to get in.'

Just then a lady with a shopping trolley and two little girls swept in through the openable door and politely held it open for the Professor, so he got in after all.

The Professor arrived at the lift, only to be met by another notice. (Ginnibag & Knitwoddle were pretty smart at notices.) It said 'We regret lift out of order.'

'Oh well, I suppose I must walk up,' said the Professor.

He went over to the stairs, but found they were cluttered up with no end of ladders, buckets and men in overalls, and another notice saying 'Stairs closed. Please use the lift.'

'But the lift is regrettably out of order,' said the Professor.

'Ah, no, sir,' said a gentleman in a pale suit and a wide smile, who seemed to be in charge of all these notices. 'That is to say we have another lift, straight through the ironmongery department.'

'Oh, um, ah, thank you,' said the Professor, but he failed to go straight through the ironmongery department because he remembered he wanted some special screws, which, as it turned out, Ginnibag & Knitwoddle were disinclined to stock.

At last the Professor got into the lift, but got out at the first floor instead of waiting for the fourth and found himself in the dress department, which was packed with so many rows of ladies' dresses, that the customers could hardly get in. And there, behind one of the rows, was Mrs Flittersnoop.

'I, um, ah, thought we were to meet in the restaurant,' said the Professor. 'I don't think they serve tea here.'

Mrs Flittersnoop was just going to answer when an extremely haughty lady with a very high hair-do swept up and asked, 'Can

I help you?' in a very well-off voice.

'Well,' said Mrs Flittersnoop, 'I was looking for a dress.'

This didn't seem to surprise tall hair-do very much as the place was stuffed tight with dresses and suits and caftans and things called separates, which you could wear one at a time or both together, according to what sort of weather it was going to be or who you were going to meet.

'Something not too expensive,' added Mrs Flittersnoop cautiously, having been slightly frightened by a price ticket she'd looked at.

'Oh, yes,' said tall hair-do in a voice that suggested Mrs Flittersnoop was a refugee from a local dustbin. She beckoned with a long skinny finger and another lady with a rather lower hair-do came up.

Professor Branestawm watched all this with professorial interest. He thought if the height of the sales ladies' hair-do's was adjusted according to the price of the dresses they sold, possibly in a sale, when things went very cheap, you might get served by a bald-headed lady, but he didn't think that would be very suitable somehow.

Meantime Mrs Flittersnoop and medium hair-do had collected a selection of dresses, and vanished with them into a little room marked 'Ladies changing room'.

Professor Branestawm was just wondering what they changed ladies into in that room and thinking he didn't want Mrs Flittersnoop changed because she suited him very well as she was, when Mrs Flittersnoop came out *very* much changed indeed. She was wearing a smart dress with a fetching pattern of coloured chains all over it.

'How do you like it, Professor?' she asked.

'Oh, um, ah, er, nice,' said the Professor, who liked the chains, but would have preferred cogwheels.

Just then a lady in a skinny little white hat emerged from the woodwork and hissed to Mrs Flittersnoop, 'Don't buy it!'

Professor Branestawm wondered if she was someone employed by Ginnibag & Knitwoddle to discourage customers from buying anything that was too cheap, so that they'd buy something more expensive. But it turned out that the lady was actually a friend of Mrs Flittersnoop's.

'Don't buy it!' she repeated. 'It's got a back zip.'

Professor Branestawm wondered what particularly vicious kind of thing a back zip could be that made it so undesirable for Mrs Flittersnoop to buy a dress that had one.

'So difficult to do up by oneself,' said the lady.

'Oh, why, yes, indeed, I'm sure,' said Mrs Flittersnoop. 'You're quite right. Never depend on others if you can help it, I always say.'

Mrs Flittersnoop couldn't bear the idea of asking Professor Branestawm to zip up her dress, so she always bought ones that did up down the front or could be put on without undoing or doing up.

Professor Branestawm stood there with his head beginning to go round and round very slowly. All this talk of back zips and separates and other ladies' dressology had so confused him that he didn't realize that an idea for a new invention had let itself into his head while he wasn't looking. It wasn't until he and Mrs Flittersnoop were seated in Ginnibag & Knitwoddle's restaurant that he realized what had happened.

'Pot of tea for two and some pastries,' said Mrs Flittersnoop to the waitress.

'I'll, um, ah, have some tomato soup,' said the Professor, forgetting it wasn't lunch-time, as he had just realized he had an invention idea rattling round inside his head.

'Zipping dresses up the back is apt to be inconvenient if you are alone. Is that not so, Mrs Flittersnoop?'

'Yes, indeed, I'm sure, sir,' said Mrs Flittersnoop. 'That's why

I've bought another dress that does up down the front.'

Just then the waitress put a bowl of tomato soup in front of the Professor, who stirred it with one of his five pairs of spectacles, put the others on, looked at the soup and said to the waitress:

'Take it away! Whoever heard of having soup at tea-time?'

Now it should have been the waitress's turn to have her head go round and round, but it didn't because she was used to dealing with rummy customers. She just took the soup away, brought the tea and pastries and Mrs Flittersnoop set about being mother, which ladies can do without having any children as long as they have a pot of tea. Then the Professor set about telling her about the idea that had come to him in the dress department for a special zip-you-up machine.

'Well, sir,' said Mrs Flittersnoop, having another jam tart, 'if I might make so bold, sir, there is already something to help you zip up a dress. It is a piece of cord with a little hook on the end. You just hook it through the tag on the zip and pull the cord over your shoulder.'

'Tut, tut,' said the Professor, putting a piece of scone into his tea in mistake for sugar. 'I don't think ladies should have to, er, mess about with bits of string in order to zip themselves up. It is not at all ladylike.'

'Well, sir,' said Mrs Flittersnoop, 'I must say I've never used one myself seeing as how I always have dresses that do up down the front.'

'With my idea,' went on the Professor, 'you have an arrangement fixed to the wall. You simply stand with your back against it, press a button and up goes your zip. Then', he took a drink of tea and two of his pairs of glasses fell into the cup, 'to unzip yourself you do exactly the same only this time the machine zips the zip down instead of up. You must, of course,' he wagged a finger and the waitress thought he wanted another scone to drop into his tea, 'you must press the button to make sure the zipping attachment is at the bottom if you wish to be zipped up, or at the top if you wish to be unzipped down, you understand?'

'Yes, indeed, I'm sure, sir,' said Mrs Flittersnoop, who didn't understand anything except that, thank goodness, she wouldn't have to use the Professor's machine as she always had button-down-the-front dresses.

Professor Branestawm was demonstrating his dress zipping and unzipping machine to the Great Pagwell Ladies' Social Club. The device was fastened to the wall where it looked something like a 'try your strength' machine that you have to hit with a hammer, something like a rather bad-tempered weighing machine, and something like the thing that tells you what the weather isn't going to be like tomorrow.

'Would some lady be kind enough to step forward so that I can demonstrate the device?' asked the Professor, looking over and under and through various pairs of spectacles.

The ladies all looked at one another and felt rather as if a conjurer was asking them to help with a trick. Nobody moved because they were all waiting for someone else to get up. Then, as nobody got up, all the ladies stood up at once, except one who was wearing a T-shirt and trousers and who couldn't therefore be zipped or unzipped up the back. They all said 'Ah!', and then sat down again.

'I, um, ah, think perhaps I might make a choice,' said the Professor, who could see the demonstration never getting off the ground, so to speak. He pointed to a young lady in a pink dress, who giggled, got up and went over to the machine. She stood with her back to it and the Professor pressed a button. There was a click.

'The zip-upping attachment has now attached itself to the tag of this lady's zip,' he explained. 'As her dress is already zipped up the machine will now unzip it.' He pressed another button, there was a whizzing sound and the young lady's nice pink dress came unzipped and fell off.

For a moment there was a moderate consternation. But as the young lady had no end of underclothes on, and as there weren't any gentlemen present, except Professor Branestawm, whose five pairs of spectacles had all fallen down over his eyes so he couldn't see anything but fog, the situation wasn't that drastic. Two other ladies helped the young lady in the pink dress, who had gone rather pink herself, back into her dress and the machine promptly zipped it up again, to a slight round of applause, though whether this was for the machine, for the Professor, or for the young lady, isn't certain.

'I, um, er, think that seems satisfactory,' said the Professor.

Then there was a rush of ladies of all kinds to try the machine. Dresses were zipped up and down with the speed of excitable lightning. And, of course, all the ladies wanted one of the Professor's remarkable self-zipping machines for themselves.

'A most satisfactory and practical invention I, um, ah, think,' said the Professor to Mrs Flittersnoop later. 'I have made my special zipping machines for the Mayoress, for Lady Pagwell, for Miss Frenzie, the Vicar's wife and many other ladies.' Maisie and Daisie said they didn't want two machines, or even one, because they could always zip each other up and down, and often wore things that didn't zip anyway.

'Yes, indeed, I'm sure, sir,' said Mrs Flittersnoop, half-wishing she had dresses that zipped up the back, so that she could have had one of the Professor's wonderful machines. But she didn't half-wish for long. Suddenly there came a ring at the door, another one on the phone and people banging on the window.

'Come quickly, Professor!' 'Help, Professor!' 'Urgent, hurry Professor!' came the demands. Panic seemed to be taking place everywhere.

At the vicarage yelps were coming from the best bedroom. The Vicar's wife was up against the ceiling, where the zipping-up machine had zipped her and wouldn't let go.

At her home Miss Frenzie was on the floor apparently looking for lost property, but in fact it was because the zipper had zipped her and her dress down on to the carpet.

At the mayoral residence the Mayoress was half way up the wall and the Mayor was all the way up it in despair.

All over Pagwell, schoolteachers, librarians, non-librarians, housewives and other assorted ladies were trapped in unladylike positions by the Professor's machines.

The Professor clapped on his hat, missed and clapped it on Mrs Flittersnoop.

'Ring up Colonel Dedshott!' gasped the Professor. 'Tell him to go and help the Mayor's wife!' He shot out and Mrs Flittersnoop got to the telephone just in time to answer a call from a lady who thought she was ringing the dairy. To save time, Mrs Flittersnoop took an order for two pints of milk, half a pint of cream, two dozen brown eggs and a white sliced loaf, then said, 'Wrong number, I'm afraid,' rang off, and got on to the Colonel.

Professor Branestawm dashed in to see Commander Hardaport (Retired), and sent him off to help Miss Frenzie, while he tore off to the rescue of the Vicar's wife. Mrs Flittersnoop rang the fire brigade and the police, and soon that half of Pagwell that wasn't on the floor or up on the ceiling in the clutches of the Professor's Zippers, was on its way to rescue those who were.

Colonel Dedshott burst into the Mayor's house waving his sword. He dashed up to the Zipper and took a swipe at it, but cut down the Mayor's new curtains instead. He jabbed at the machine again, and the Mayor's wife shot up the rest of the way to the ceiling, shook down a yard of plaster and came down with a wallop, complete with machine and some of the wall.

Commander Hardaport, hard at rescuing Miss Frenzie

managed to get the Professor's Zipper to shoot up, but it took Miss Frenzie with it. The Commander shouted nautical commands and pressed buttons. Miss Frenzie came down again and shot up to the ceiling once more.

'Avast there!' shouted the Commander.

Miss Frenzie did three more ups and downs before the Commander managed to disentangle her from the machine and stop it with a sharp kick that hurt him more than it did the machine, as he wasn't wearing his sea boots.

The Professor was having trouble with the Vicar's wife who was still up against the ceiling. He fiddled with the machine. The Vicar's wife came down with a run on top of him. The Professor pressed the machine button and the Vicar's wife went sailing up again accompanied by the Professor, whose coat had got caught in her zip.

All over Pagwell the Zipper Rescue Operations were going on. Firemen were failing to rescue schoolteachers; the Catapult Cavaliers were unsuccessful in rescuing librarians; hospital orderlies had no chance of rescuing non-librarians, and policemen were being arrested by bad-tempered zipping machines and imprisoned on ceilings accompanied by ladies they hardly knew.

But at last it was over. The Professor's machines were subdued, busted-up, collapsed or otherwise dealt with. Ginnibag & Knitwoddle did a roaring trade in button-down-the-front dresses from zipper-allergic ladies, while other ladies made up their minds to make do with wire coat-hangers suitably manipulated to zip themselves up and down in comparative safety.

But the Professor's Zipper produced one happy ending. A young policeman got married to a rather attractive girl librarian, whom he'd met in the zipper when they got fixed together, and he had proposed to her on the seventeenth trip up to the ceiling.

10

The Great Cake Scandal

If the vicarage sale of work had been held on Friday the thirteenth instead of Saturday the fourteenth, it might have been luckier in some ways. But in Pagwell things happen like that, possibly because Professor Branestawm lives there.

Mrs Flittersnoop was elbow-deep in cooking. She wore her apron inside out, which sounds rather the sort of thing Professor Branestawm might have done himself if he ever did any cooking, which he didn't. Thank goodness, perhaps. But Mrs Flittersnoop found the pockets more convenient that way, and if she spilt anything on the apron it didn't show on the right side. Ladies can be very ingenious if they try.

Mrs Flittersnoop always baked a cake on Friday and she used to put it in the oven half an hour before her sister Aggie in Lower Pagwell used to ring up. Sister Aggie always rang up on Fridays at eleven o'clock while she had her elevenses, to talk to Mrs Flittersnoop about her bunions. And Mrs Flittersnoop used to time her cake by sister Aggie's bunion talk, which worked very well, as sister Aggie was a very consistent talker and her bunions were always very reliable.

But this Friday, Mrs Flittersnoop was baking a special cake for the vicarage sale of work, so she put it in the oven rather later so as to be sure sister Aggie would have rung off before the cooker rang up to say the cake was done. But, oh dear! This week sister Aggie had an extra bunion to talk about, also an argument with the milkman who had left the wrong coloured eggs, not to mention a few bits of extra gossip about the neighbours. So the talk went on much longer than usual. Mrs Flittersnoop's cooker went 'ting', meaning 'Your cake's done', but sister Aggie was still in full flow. And the telephone was in the hall, too far from the kitchen to reach the cooker and switch it off. So the highly special cake for the vicarage sale of work was burnt as successfully as King Alfred could have done it.

'Oh dear, good gracious me, I'm sure!' cried Mrs Flittersnoop, opening the kitchen window and letting out clouds of cake smoke, which might have dirtied next-door's washing, only it wasn't next-door's washing day. 'Oh dear!' she wailed. 'Now what am I going to do? I can't send a burnt cake to the sale of work.'

'Why not bake another one?' suggested Professor Branestawm, feeling no end practical.

'I can't,' said Mrs Flittersnoop. 'I haven't got any flour and I've run out of currants.'

'I'll pop out and get some more,' offered the Professor, getting more practical every minute, which wasn't a bit like him, but perhaps the burnt cake smoke had got at him.

'Thank you kindly, I'm sure, sir,' said Mrs Flittersnoop. 'But today's early closing, which means that the shops are shut all day since they brought in the new rules about extra shopping time.'

'Ah,' said the Professor, his brains beginning to whiz a bit, 'I wish I could invent you a cake in my inventory, but I am afraid it would not be, um, ah, very eatable.'

'No, I'm sure it wouldn't,' said Mrs Flittersnoop, then she suddenly got an idea. Living with the Professor you were apt to catch ideas as other people catch measles, only, fortunately, they didn't give you spots.

'If you were to make an imitation cake, sir,' she said, 'you could take it along to the sale of work, then wait until the sale opened and buy it back. That way nobody would know it wasn't a real cake.'

'Um, ah, oh, yes, excellent!' said the Professor, rather wishing

Mrs Flittersnoop wouldn't keep having better ideas than he had himself. But he shot into his inventory and presently came out with his imitation cake, made of goodness-knows-what, but looking very convincing.

'Lovely!' cried Mrs Flittersnoop. 'It looks just like a real cake. Nobody will ever know. Now off you go, sir, and don't forget, you must wait until the sale of work opens and buy that cake back before anyone else does.'

'Yes, yes, of course,' said the Professor and off he set, actually taking the cake to the sale and not a pair of shoes to be mended, or a library book to be exchanged, by mistake.

He handed the cake in to the Vicar, took a walk round the hall where the sale of work was being held, and the moment the Mayor declared the sale open, the Professor shot up to the cake stand, pointed to his imitation cake and said:

'I'll buy that, please!'

'Oh, I'm afraid you can't do that,' said the lady in charge of the stand. 'It's going to be raffled. But you can buy a ticket, of course.'

'Tut, tut,' said the Professor. 'I've taken a fancy to that cake and I particularly want to buy it.'

'Well, you could buy several tickets to give you a better chance,' said the lady.

The Professor's brains shot into top gear and revved up. 'That is an excellent, um, ah, idea,' he said. 'I will buy several tickets. In fact I will buy all the tickets and so make sure of getting the cake.'

'Oh, I don't know that you can do that,' said the lady.

'Why, of course he can,' said the lady on the home-made jellies stand next door. 'It doesn't matter who buys the tickets, and if this gentleman wants to buy them all, why shouldn't he?'

So the Professor bought all the tickets and held out his hand for the cake.

'Oh, you can't take it now!' said the lady. 'You must wait for the draw. The Mayor is going to draw the tickets and announce the winner this afternoon. You come back then and get the cake.'

Waiting for the afternoon, of course, would take a bit of time, so the Professor went home and explained things to Mrs Flittersnoop, who said he was to be sure and be there when the Mayor made the draw so as to be certain of getting the cake.

At last afternoon came, and the Professor got back to the hall in time for the draw. The Mayor put his hand into a waste-paper basket containing the tickets for the cake raffle, drew one out and said:

'I have pleasure in announcing the result of the cake raffle. It is', he peered at the ticket, 'Mrs Slumpton.'

'No, no, no!' cried the Professor. 'There must be some mistake.'

There was. The Professor was attending the raffle for the wrong cake. He shot round the sale of work. Cake and jelly and marmalade and crocheted doily raffles were going on all over the place. But at last he tracked down the lady he bought his tickets from, just as that raffle was being drawn. The Mayoress drew out a ticket. It had Professor Branestawm's name on it; he took the cake and rushed off home with it.

'Well, thank goodness, indeed, I'm sure, sir,' said Mrs Flittersnoop.

She unwrapped the cake, let out a shriek and collapsed on a kitchen chair, which was a lot too hard for collapsing on with any degree of comfort.

'This isn't *our* cake, sir!' she cried.

It certainly wasn't. It was a real cake, not a bit like the Professor's imitation one. With all those raffles going on and people surging about buying things and looking at things, the cakes must have got mixed up.

'Oh dear!' cried Mrs Flittersnoop. 'Whatever shall we do?

Somebody will buy that imitation cake and think I did it.'

'I don't see how they can know that,' said the Professor. 'It didn't have your name on it.'

'No, sir, but you took the cake in, so they'll guess it was one of mine.'

'I'll dash back and buy our one,' said the Professor, 'if I can find out who's got it.'

'I'll make a cup of tea for you first, sir,' said Mrs Flittersnoop, 'and you may as well have a slice of this cake with it, to keep your strength up.'

She put the cake on a plate and stuck a knife in it.

Pop, pouff. There was a most un-cake like noise and the cake collapsed. Mrs Flittersnoop cut a piece out and there was a punctured balloon inside it.

'It looks to, um, ah, me', said the Professor, 'as if someone else has had a spot of trouble with their cake.'

'Oh dear, never mind about that!' cried Mrs Flittersnoop, going up in dithers. 'You must rush back to the sale of work and find out who has bought our cake and get it back, sir.'

The Professor was just about to shoot off when Mrs Flittersnoop called out, 'Wait a minute, sir. I think you'd better take this cake back with you, as the person who made it will probably want to buy it back, so that nobody will know.'

'Just as we did,' said the Professor, who was quick at understanding things, being a Professor and plentifully brainy.

'Why, yes, indeed, I'm sure, sir,' said Mrs Flittersnoop. 'It's a pity I've cut it, but I'll just put the piece back and wrap it up. Then you can take it back, find out who has got ours and hope for the best.'

The Professor shot off and Mrs Flittersnoop went into the kitchen to hope for the best.

Back at the sale the Professor fought his way through the jellies and marmalade and crocheted doilies to the cake stall, gave them the balloon cake, said, 'Please sell this again for the funds,' and disappeared in search of the Vicar.

'Who won Mrs Flittersnoop's cake?' he panted.

'Why you did, sir,' said the lady in charge of the raffle. 'You bought all the tickets, so you had to win.'

'Yes, yes, but no, no!' cried the Professor. 'There has been a mistake. Someone else got it, and I must find out who it is.'

'Dear me,' said the Vicar. 'I trust there was nothing wrong with the cake? I believe it was won by Mrs Trumpington-Smawl.'

'Good gracious!' cried the Professor. He dashed out, dashed home and dashed into his special motor car, dashed out in it, dashed the wrong way, dashed round and dashed off again.

'Oh, dear me, I'm sure!' wailed Mrs Flittersnoop, whom he'd managed to tell about it between dashes. 'Mrs Trumpington-Smawl is a very haughty lady, I'm afraid. If she gets that imitation cake of the Professor's, she'll go on like anything.'

Meantime the Professor was going on like anything. He forgot where Mrs Trumpington-Smawl lived, asked a policeman who didn't know, remembered where it was, but forgot how to get there, but at last he arrived, shot out of his car and knocked at the door.

'I'm, um, ah, afraid I hardly know what to say to the lady,' he thought. 'She is not the kind of person who will hand over a cake she has won without wanting to know a great many reasons why she should, and the only reason I can give her is one I dare not.'

Fortunately Mrs Trumpington-Smawl was out.

The Professor crept round to the back and looked through the kitchen window.

Ha! There on the table was his imitation cake, unwrapped but fortunately no attempt had been made to cut it.

'Just in time,' breathed the Professor.

Luckily Mrs Trumpington-Smawl had left the window open a bit for her cats to pop in and out. The Professor opened it wider, crept in and picked up the cake. Immediately Mrs Trumpington-Smawl's cats leapt on him and started to wash, as they preferred washing on people rather than on the sideboard, or the mantelpiece or the top of the wardrobe, as those were places where they liked to sleep.

'I, oh, ah, um, dear me!' gasped the Professor, trying to scrape the cats off himself, but they were highly tenacious cats and it took a bit of doing. But at last he managed it, grabbed the cake, climbed out of the window and made a dash for his car.

But no sooner had he shaken off the cats than he ran into a policeman.

'Ah now,' said the policeman in a very dark blue voice with stripes in it. 'What would you be doing running out of this house with a cake, may I ask?'

The Professor explained, but his explanation was so complicated the policeman's head began to go round and round. This made his helmet feel rather uncomfortable, so he decided to take the Professor to the police station and let the sergeant's head go round and round instead.

'So you made an imitation cake and passed it off as a real one, did you,' said the sergeant, writing like mad in a book. 'That would be an offence against the Trade Descriptions Act of what's-its-name, paragraph thingummy, section so and so.'

'No, no, no!' cried the Professor. 'I bought the cake back or at least I bought all the raffle tickets to make sure of winning it.'

'Ha, cheating at gambling,' said the sergeant, writing a lot more. 'That's another offence you know. Really this takes the cake.'

Those words gave the Professor an idea. He snatched up the cake, dodged the policeman, shot out of the police station and started to run home, but unfortunately he ran into Mrs

Trumpington-Smawl on the way.

'Oh, my dear Professor,' she said in a very stuck-up voice. 'Why, you've got my cake back. Someone stole it from my kitchen while I was out and evidently the police caught the thief. So kind of you to collect it for me.' And she took the cake from the Professor and swept off.

But Mrs Flittersnoop wasn't the only person in Pagwell who had had problems with her baking that day.

Earlier that morning the Mayoress took out of the oven the cake she was baking for the vicarage sale, looked at it as if she hadn't been introduced and said in a rather sniffy voice:

'Not up to my usual standard, I fear.'

'Oh, I think it looks lovely,' said her friend Lilly Lopley, who was staying with her.

'It may be good enough for some people,' said Mrs Mayor in a very elevated voice, 'but I demand perfection. However', she went on, 'there isn't time to make another one so it will have to do, but I should be extremely obliged Lilly if you'd buy it back as soon as the sale opens. I don't want people thinking my cake baking is going off.'

So Lilly said all right and she went off to the sale, and in due time came back with a parcel.

'Oh really, that is most inconvenient!' exclaimed Mrs Mayor as she undid the wrappings. 'This is not my cake you have bought, Lilly. How could you be so careless?'

'Well, I bought it from the same person I gave yours to,' said Lilly. 'They must have got things mixed, a sort of cake mixture, you know,' and she giggled a giggle that Mrs Mayor instantly froze with a spiky glance.

'Well!' she exclaimed.

It wasn't at all well, of course, because people never say that if it is.

The cake was made of sawdust and putty.

Mrs Hokkibats sent in some doughnuts which were quite uneatable but bounced rather well, so she tried to buy them back to use as tennis balls, as she and her husband were dotty about games. But they were won in another raffle by Commander Hardaport (Retired), who thought they were cannonballs but reckoned they were a bit out of date for modern warships that prefer playing with guided missiles.

Miss Frenzie set out to make a shattering cake from her latest recipe, but it went a bit wonky because Lord Pagwell, her boss, called her away at a vital moment.

So she sent the cake along with Violet and gave her strict instructions to buy it back the moment the sale opened.

But when Violet returned and they unwrapped the cake and tried to cut it to have a slice with their tea, it broke the knife.

'This isn't my cake!' shrieked Miss Frenzie. 'I told you to buy my cake back, but you got the wrong one.'

'They all looked alike when they were wrapped up,' said Violet.

It was evidently an unlucky day for cakes, the sun being in the seventh quarter of Capricorn, or Venus not rising at the right time, or Aquarius drying up, or the weather being too damp or not warm enough, or the gas and electricity companies messing about. Or else some of the Pagwell housewives had been getting their centigrades mixed up with their fahrenheits, or their kilos confused with their pounds, their litres with their pints and their grammes with their ounces.

Every single one of the disastrous cakes had been bought by ladies who hadn't made them. And every single one of the ladies, some of whom weren't single but married, were trying to get back their own cakes. Mrs Trumpington-Smawl had the Professor's, Miss Frenzie had Mrs Trumpington-Smawl's, and the Doctor's wife had Miss Frenzie's.

Then there was a lot more rushing to and fro as all the ladies wrapped up the cakes they'd got, took them back to the sale of work and tried to buy back their own cakes again. But they only got in a worse muddle than before.

The score now stood as follows:

Mrs Trumpington-Smawl had Miss Frenzie's cake.

Miss Frenzie had the Mayoress's.

The Mayoress had the Doctor's wife's.

The Doctor's wife had Mrs Hokkibats's doughnuts.

The Vicar had the trembles, the megrims and the dithers, not knowing what was going on, but realizing it was something inappropriate.

Then all the ladies went rushing back yet again to have another go at retrieving their cakes. But the people at the sale were very conscientious and as soon as a cake was brought back to be sold again they gift-wrapped it, so all the cakes looked alike and nobody could tell which was theirs. But it was nice for the sale of work, because the same cakes kept getting bought, brought back, bought again, brought back and bought once more. It was awful, really, as none of the cakes were worth buying. But then they were being bought by the people who'd made a mess of them, so perhaps that was poetic thingummy.

'Well!' said Mrs Flittersnoop. 'At least I'm not the only one to send an unsatisfactory cake to the sale. Whoever had to stuff theirs with a balloon can't say anything about my, or rather *your*, imitation one, Professor.'

The Mayor's wife was also mollified by the thought that even if her cake wasn't one hundred and ten per cent perfect as she'd wanted it, at least someone else had made a much worse one.

Miss Frenzie reckoned her wonky cake was at least better than the disastrous one Violet had brought back.

In fact the only person who got a decent cake out of the sale was Lady Pagwell, who eventually got the Mayor's wife's not quite perfect cake, which was actually very good. But Lady Pagwell was trying to slim, so she didn't eat any.

But for a long time after that none of the ladies of Great Pagwell would accept invitations to one another's houses for tea in case they got given a frightful cake. So Ye Olde Bunne Shoppe did a roaring trade in tea parties, because you could be reasonably certain of not finding popped balloons or sawdust or anything else irregular in their cakes.

Mrs Flittersnoop actually had nothing to worry about because, although Mrs Trumpington-Smawl had very nearly blown her top when she'd got the Professor's cake home again and found it was an imitation one, she rather guessed what had happened.

'Only one person in this town could possibly have made a cake like this,' she sniffed. 'And that is Professor Branestawm. But why he should have sent it to the sale of work is more than I can imagine. Poor Mrs Flittersnoop must have spent a lot of time and thought making one of her nice cakes for the sale and the Professor probably made that imitation one for a display and got them mixed up.'

And the Vicar, who'd had a bit of a time trying to sort out the various excitable ladies and their cakes, decided that the next sale of work would be for nice innocent things like knitting and embroidery and woollen bedsocks that weren't likely to cause social commotions in Pagwell.

11

The Invention that Was too Successful

Colonel Dedshott knocked on the door. Mrs Flittersnoop opened it. Colonel Dedshott saluted, clicked his heels and said:

'Morning. Professor in? What, hrrrm, ha!'

'Good morning, I'm sure, sir,' said Mrs Flittersnoop. 'You'll find him in his inventory, sir.' And she went back to the kitchen to switch the iron off and switch the kettle on, ready to make coffee for the Professor and the Colonel.

But although Mrs Flittersnoop had told the Colonel he'd find the Professor in his inventory, he couldn't find him. There was nobody in sight and nowhere big enough for the Professor to hide. Not that he was given to hiding and popping out and saying boo, as this isn't the sort of thing professors care much about doing.

'You there, Branestawm, what?' called the Colonel. 'My goodness, by Jove!' The last bit was because the Professor had suddenly appeared from nowhere. There he was standing in a strange open cupboard affair.

'Ah, Dedshott,' he said, 'I'm glad you were able to come. I'd like you to see a new invention of mine that will revolutionize warfare.'

'Hrrm,' replied the Colonel, not feeling sure if he wanted warfare revolutionized in case it meant abolishing colonels, or not having any horses, or refusing to fight the enemy in case it wasn't polite.

'Camouflage,' said the Professor, dropping three pairs of spectacles, which vanished under the work-bench.

'But I say, Branestawm, you know,' protested the Colonel, screwing his moustache up a bit tighter, 'you can't invent camouflage. Been done already, y'know. Army already using it.'

'Tut, tut, yes, I know,' said the Professor, raking his three pairs of spectacles from under the bench and dropping the other two in a glue-pot that was fortunately empty. 'I don't mean the ordinary sort of um, ah, camouflage. Vehicles painted in dirty brown and green patches to match the countryside. All very well in the right sort of country, but what about in towns? Camouflaged, um, ah, tanks going down a street look very, er, um, obvious painted to look like trees and bushes.'

'Ha, yes, by Jove!' said the Colonel. 'But if you paint 'em to look like houses, they'll stick out in the country, y'know. Enemy spot 'em in a moment.'

'Precisely,' said the Professor. 'That is why I have developed an entirely new kind of camouflage. Or at least I have developed an old idea for making things invisible. It is, ah, used very successfully by magicians.'

'My word!' exclaimed the Colonel. 'You don't mean spells and incantations, Branestawm? Black magic and all that, what!'

'No, no, not as old as all that,' said the Professor, sweeping the Colonel's hat off the work-bench to make room for the coffee Mrs Flittersnoop had just brought in. 'Mirrors, my dear Dedshott, diverse formation, transparent reflectors and other devices employed by conjurers and illusionists.'

He poured out two cups of coffee, gave the coffee pot to the Colonel, handed the cups to Mrs Flittersnoop and went on.

'This cabinet from which I appeared so, um, ah, dramatically and startled you just now,' he said, pointing to the open cupboard. 'I was in there all the time, but a mirror reflected the side of the cabinet so that you thought you were looking at the back of it, when really you were looking at a mirror that was concealing me.'

'Ha, my word!' said the Colonel, putting down the coffee pot and taking the cups of coffee from Mrs Flittersnoop, who escaped to her ironing in case the Professor started concealing it behind mirrors.

'I am developing a system of illusionary methods,' continued the Professor, 'by which, with the use of mirrors, transparent reflectors, background work and other methods, I can cause a vehicle, such as an, um, ah, tank, to appear invisible by reflecting its surroundings much as the mirror in the cupboard concealed me.'

'Ha, my word, jolly clever!' said the Colonel, wondering how a tank could appear invisible, because if it appeared it couldn't be invisible, but he knew better than to argue with the Professor. Anyway his head was going round and round as it always did when listening to the Professor's explanations and he found it difficult to drink his coffee without getting it in his ears.

The Professor picked up a piece of looking-glass.

'Here is a practical, um, ah, demonstration,' he said. 'Come into the garden.'

They went outside and the Professor held the edge of the looking-glass at right angles against a hedge, then he stood behind the looking-glass. 'If you will be good enough to stand over there,' he said to the Colonel, 'you will see that part of me has vanished.'

The Colonel looked and gasped. A slice of the Professor's middle had vanished completely.

'You think you can see the hedge through me,' said the Professor, 'but actually the mirror is reflecting another part of the hedge and you see that instead of me. You see what this means!' he said, and the Colonel, who by now couldn't see what anything meant, said, 'By Jove, yes, what!'

'Tanks can be made invisible,' said the Professor. 'Armoured cars can vanish, troop carriers can be unseen. The enemy will be unable to see us, and victory in the case of war will be easy. I can adapt my new illusionistic camouflage by means of mirrors, background masking, diverse formation and other devices. The mirrors can be made to move, activated by the light, so that they reflect wherever necessary to make the vehicle invisible. And', the Professor waved his arms in circles, 'when the tanks and other vehicles are moving, the resultant movement of the surroundings reflected in the mirror will appear to be the natural effect of wind.'

'But what about the noise of engines?' asked the Colonel. 'No use being invisible if you can hear 'em, what.'

'Oh, indeed,' said the Professor. 'But that is no, um, ah, problem. I have devised a method of reducing the sound of the engines to almost nothing. But in any case,' he pointed at the Colonel with a handful of spectacles, 'even if the enemy could hear the sound of the engines, they would be puzzled to know what it was since they could see nothing.'

The Colonel's head was going round so fast he couldn't say anything.

'I must see General Shatterfortz at once!' said the Professor, grabbing his hat and putting it on the Colonel's head.

'Ha, my word, yes,' said the Colonel, dashing after the Professor. 'But better not tell him too much. He'll never believe you can make invisible tanks, y'know. Too much for him to grasp. Can't grasp it meself.'

'No, no, yes, yes,' said the Professor. 'I'll tell him just enough about my new illusionistic camouflage to get him interested, and let the rest be a surprise.'

'Not a word of this must leak out, y'know,' said General Shatterfortz, when the Professor told him of his invention. 'Deadly secret and all that. No public demonstrations. Very hush-hush. I'll call a secret meeting of the Military.'

He called it, in a whisper of course, and the highly secret, frightfully hush-hush, meeting of high-up Army types took place in a disused Bingo Hall scheduled for demolition with 'Danger

Keep Out' notices all over the place. Everybody wrote with soft pencils, so that pen-scratching noises shouldn't be heard. Tea was served in silent rubber teacups, and, in case reporters asked awkward questions, the newspapers were told that the meeting was to decide whether or not soldiers should wear long pants in the winter.

At last, when all the rubber teacups had been used up and the soft pencils worn down, it was agreed that Professor Branestawm should supervise the building of several of his invisible tanks and armoured cars.

'The men who are building them must be sworn to secrecy, y'know,' said General Shatterfortz.

It was all very difficult and took a long time because the men had to talk in whispers, and hammers had to be padded and electric drills made noiseless so that nobody should know what was going on. But at last the Professor's wonderful illusionistic camouflaged vehicles were ready.

General Shatterfortz, Colonel Dedshott, several highly important ministers and, of course, Professor Branestawm, stood in a little tent at the edge of a large piece of country that the Army had rather forcibly borrowed from Pagwell Council for a demonstration of the Professor's vehicles. Nobody else was allowed within miles of the place. Even cows were excluded, as they are rather apt to be inquisitive.

'Let the demonstration commence!' commanded General Shatterfortz.

Nothing happened.

'Hrrrrmph,' said Colonel Dedshott.

'What's this, y'know?' demanded the General. 'Where's the demonstration? Someone filled in the wrong form? Can't have, we didn't allow forms.'

Professor Branestawm smiled and said nothing.

A great deal more nothing happened.

'Something gone wrong with your invention, I suppose,' grunted the General. 'Got a good explanation for it, I expect. Good gracious!'

The last remark was sparked off by a series of loud bangs and puffs of smoke from all over the surrounding countryside.

'The tanks are opening, um, ah, fire,' said the Professor.

Several more bangs occurred and puffs of smoke took place in a line in front of the General.

'Don't understand it,' he grunted. 'What is it, land mines? Where are your confounded tanks and things?'

'That is them,' said the Professor, talking very ungrammatically because he was slightly excited. 'Those are my tanks firing blanks. The tanks are invisible because of my new illusionistic camouflage.'

'Fiddlesticks!' cried the General.

'Ah,' said the Professor. 'We did not tell you everything about my invention, General, because, as you said, it had to be kept very secret. You didn't expect to see tanks that were invisible, did you?'

'Couldn't very well see 'em if they were,' grunted the General. 'Thought your new camouflage would make 'em difficult to spot, but this is ridiculous! Don't believe it. You haven't got any tanks there. It's some trick or other.'

'Come with me,' said the Professor and he took the General, followed by the others, across a field.

'Ow!' said the General, which was a very unmilitary thing for him to say, but he'd stubbed his toe on something.

It was a tank.

'Put out your hands,' said the Professor. 'You can feel it, even if you can't see it.'

And, sure enough, the General found there was a tank there and now, being very close, he could just see it, with mirrors bristling out at all angles, panes of glass shifting and revolving,

gadgets of all kinds twiddling about and reflecting the surroundings so that the tank itself couldn't be seen.

'Amazing, y'know,' said the General, when they got back to the Professor's house. The invisible tanks had been dismissed to their secret hiding-places which, of course, could have been anywhere as they were invisible anyway.

'Puts Britain in the forefront of military preparedness,' said the General, as Mrs Flittersnoop put some cups of tea and home-made cakes in the forefront of the General and the others.

'Difficulty is', said the General, 'country can't reward you with proper recognition, y'know. Mean to say give you knighthood, elevate you to peerage. Wouldn't do. Have to say what it was done for and that would give away secret.'

'Oh, um, ah, that's quite all right,' said the Professor, who didn't fancy being elevated to anything in case he fell off. And Mrs Flittersnoop felt rather glad the Professor wasn't going to be knighted because she wouldn't have known whether to call him Sir Professor or Sir Branestawm or what.

'All the same,' said the General, 'you have the satisfaction of knowing you have done great service to your country. Bravo!' He took another of Mrs Flittersnoop's cakes, raised his teacup and said, 'Here's a toast to Britain's hero, Professor Branestawm.'

'Here! Here!' cried the others, and Mrs Flittersnoop, who thought they were calling for more tea and cakes, made a fresh pot and brought out another plateful.

'I'm so glad your invention was a success, sir, I'm sure,' said Mrs Flittersnoop later on. 'But what a pity it must be so secret. Still I always think it's nice to know you've accomplished something, even if the papers don't talk about it.'

But alas and alack, and oh dearie me, the Professor hadn't put Britain in the forefront of military preparedness. He'd put General Shatterfortz in a highly awkward position.

The Professor's marvellous, highly successful, utterly amazing invisible tanks and armoured cars were the secret successful failure of the century. They were a catastrophe of enormous dimensions.

But why? Weren't they sufficiently invisible? Could they be detected if looked at through smoked spectacles? Could thunderstorms, or bright sunshine, or heavy showers expose them?

No, no, definitely, no. They were invisible all right. The Professor's illusionistic principles worked perfectly.

That was the trouble. The Professor's invention was too successful by three-quarters and a bit. The vehicles were completely invisible under all conditions and wherever they went. But, and it was a but ten times higher than the Post Office Tower, although the enemy couldn't see them, they couldn't see each other either. The Army didn't know where their tanks were. Nobody could see them.

Lady motorists ran into them in the High Street. Gentlemen motorists ran into them on motorways. They caused invisible traffic jams.

And the soldiers who worked the tanks and armoured cars got unscrupulous ideas. They took unauthorized tea-breaks. Some of them went for seaside holidays in their tanks. Seaside towns were startled out of their sun-tans by the sudden appearance from nowhere of bunches of soldiers demanding fish and chips, while the invisible tanks got in the way of carnival processions.

General Shatterfortz was stamping up and down his office with smoke coming out of his ears. He didn't know where his armoured forces were or how to get hold of them. He sent radio messages to them saying, 'Come in number four!' and so on, as if they were hired rowing boats whose time was up. But the invisible tanks didn't answer, because the soldiers were either deep in tea or on holiday at Blackpool.

Fortunately for the General, before the War Office got to hea of it, which naturally took some time as Government Depart ments are always slow at hearing about things, the soldier finished their tea-breaks, or got tired of their seaside holidays and came back, still invisible, to report for duty.

'Now, Professor,' said General Shatterfortz, 'I must ask you t supervise the de-invisibling of these vehicles so that the Army ca get back to normal, y'know.'

But whether the Army ever did get back to normal, or indee whether they even knew where it was, nobody will ever know.

12

The Branestawm Church Service

Professor Branestawm was immersed in Christmas card sending. And he was doing it most methodically.

'I, um, ah, must take care not to get things muddled up,' he said to Mrs Flittersnoop. 'It wouldn't do at all for our friends to get the wrong cards or not get them at all.'

'Yes indeed, I'm sure, sir,' said Mrs Flittersnoop, who'd had an exceedingly rowdy card from the Professor last Christmas because he'd picked up two at once in the shop by mistake, and had put the wrong one back without noticing.

'To make sure I don't forget to post them,' he said, 'I am going to address one to myself. Then when that arrives it will do two things, it will show that I have posted the others and it will remind me not to post another lot.'

Mrs Flittersnoop had nothing to say to that, as she'd had to go and answer the door. Not that the door was in the habit of asking questions, but the bell had just rung, which meant someone had called.

It turned out to be the Vicar with smiles and good wishes and a calendar with a picture of Great Pagwell Church.

'Ah, good morning, Professor,' said the Vicar, 'I wonder if I might take advantage of your most ingenious mind to help me solve a rather awkward problem connected with the church. You were so successful in dealing with the vicarage tree, I'd hoped you could help me again.'

'Ah yes,' said the Professor. He sometimes had awkward problems connected with the church himself, because when he went there with Mrs Flittersnoop he always got so interested in working out complicated mathematical sums with the numbers on the hymn board that he found himself a bit out of step with the service. If he knelt down, he found everyone else standing up, and when he stood up, everyone else sat down. Then when the plate came round he was apt to say, 'Oh, ah, thank you,' and take a coin and try to eat it, thinking he was at a party and snacks were being handed round. But he was only too pleased for people to take advantage of his most ingenious mind, though it was by no means certain that it would solve problems, awkward or otherwise. In fact, it was much more likely to create them. But this didn't seem to deter the Vicar, who was professionally good at having faith in people and he had great faith in the Professor, though goodness knows why.

Mrs Flittersnoop found some suitable organ music on the radio, while the Vicar explained his problem to the Professor.

'People are not coming to church enough,' he said. 'That is to say not enough of them are coming to church, if you follow me.'

'Ah,' said the Professor, 'but if people follow you they will undoubtedly come to church, will they not?'

The radio changed over from a deeply religious oratorio to a programme of Hot Spot Pop Tops.

'Ah, yes, indeed,' said the Vicar. 'But the fact remains Great Pagwell Church is half empty for the services.'

'Well,' said the Professor, 'that means it is half full, which isn't bad.'

'Ah, but not good enough, I fear,' said the Vicar, while Mrs Flittersnoop smothered The Flaming Friends pop group on the radio and brought in cups of coffee and little cakes arranged in a cross on the plate to make them look suitable for the Vicar.

'We want the church filled,' went on the Vicar, 'but the trouble is my parish is so extensive, people have rather a long way to go so they tend to stop at home and listen to services on the radio, which I am afraid does very little good to our collection for the building fund to enlarge the church.'

'But why enlarge the church if you don't, um, ah, get enough people to fill it?' asked the Professor.

'One must move with the times,' answered the Vicar, 'and hope that in due course more people will be attracted to the church. Then it would be a great pity, nay almost a disaster, if the church were not big enough to accommodate them.'

'Um, ah, now, Vicar,' said Professor Branestawm, arranging his five pairs of spectacles in their best thinking order, 'you say it is too far for people to go to your church. Then why not take your church to the people?'

'Dear me,' laughed the Vicar. 'I fear it is rather too immovable for that.'

'A travelling church!' said the Professor, waving his hands and making the Vicar's coffee go cold. 'Something to go round and round-up the non-church-goers,' he went on. 'You must do a little recruiting, Vicar. Go out and persuade them that your church is worth a little trouble to visit. I will look into the matter and see what I can invent.'

'That is most kind of you,' said the Vicar and he went out saying two small prayers, one of thanks for being able to get the Professor to help and another of hope that the Professor's help wouldn't turn out more disastrous than usual.

Professor Branestawm saw him out, and then went out himself to post his Christmas cards.

'Dear me, here's one addressed to me,' he said, finding the one he'd addressed to himself. 'How silly of me.' So he left it behind and posted the others.

When he got back home, he went into his inventory to invent a travelling church in which the Vicar could tour his parish to round-up radio-listening parishioners and get them to come to his live three-dimensional church in the round, so to speak.

*

One week and several inventions later the Professor came down to breakfast and asked:

'Is there a Christmas card for me from myself?'

Mrs Flittersnoop said there wasn't.

'Ah,' said the Professor and the complicated explanations began. 'That means I forgot to post the Christmas cards to the other people we want to send them to. You see, I sent one to myself, so that if it arrived I'd know I'd posted the others, but if it didn't that would mean I had forgotten to post the rest. Well it hasn't come, so I didn't post them and we must send them now.'

So he and Mrs Flittersnoop addressed another lot of cards and Mrs Flittersnoop posted them herself this time to make sure. But since the Professor had already posted the other cards, though not the one to himself, everyone got two cards from him. But they reckoned that was the sort of thing the Professor might do, so everything was all right after all, and the Professor went back to inventing his travelling church, while the Vicar went on preaching long sermons to very short congregations.

At last the Branestawm Travelling Church was finished. It looked rather like a caravan with stained glass windows and a steeple. It had a pulpit for preaching recruiting sermons from. It had an organ that played rousing hymns, a peal of bells to bring the people along to hear the sermons, and over the pulpit an angel with a trumpet instead of a horn.

'Bless me!' exclaimed the Vicar when he saw it. 'I, er, really do not know what the Bishop will say about this.'

But the Bishop, who had an urgent date to confirm a clump of schoolchildren before they grew up too much, didn't say anything, though he did wonder rather a lot.

'I will accompany you on your first round,' said the Professor. 'Show you how everything works.'

They got in. The Professor pressed a button and the organ

started playing the can-can. The Professor hurriedly switched over to 'O Come, All Ye Faithful' and drove off, just missing a number $38\frac{1}{2}$ bus, which he didn't want to catch anyway.

The mobile church went humming and hymning along Church Street, down Temple Lane, past several cross roads, through Noel Street, Parish Lane, Bell Avenue, and Spire Lane, until the Vicar called, 'Stop here! This is a good rural spot.'

It was Pagwell Halfpenny, certainly rural but not very hopeful-sounding for collections.

'Now, let us see if we get a congregation,' said the Vicar. 'I think we might give a peal or two on the bells to attract the populace.'

The Professor pulled levers and the bells rang out *ding dong, dong ding, dong dong*, as bells like doing.

'Ah, here they come,' said the Vicar.

The first lot was a group of little boys who thought the Travelling Church was an ice cream van, but the Vicar couldn't even offer them a sundae, which seems strange. Then a pretty girl asked the Professor if he would marry her. But she had mistaken him for the Vicar, and what she really meant was that she wanted him to marry her to someone else. Several very country ladies thought the Travelling Church was a travelling supermarket and arrived with baskets, hoping to get groceries at something off, but only got the Vicar's recruiting sermon which went on and on.

Another lady brought her baby along to be christened, but, alas, there was no font in the caravan, not even a kitchen sink, as the Professor hadn't thought it would be needed. Someone suggested holding the baby's head under the village drinking fountain, but the Vicar hurriedly began another sermon.

They did rather better at their next stop, which was Pagwell Hassett, and better still at Pagwell-under-Water, and, by the time they got to Pagwell-in-the-Maze, people were queuing up to hear the Vicar.

'Well, I think our mission has been very successful,' beamed the Vicar when they got back.

Next Sunday his church had even fewer people than usual.

'I really don't understand it,' he said.

Soon the Travelling Church was doing a roaring service. People were queuing to attend it, and the Vicar added to his sermon a few choice hymns.

'But this is really ridiculous!' he cried. 'People are going to the Travelling Church, but they aren't coming here to the main church.'

'I, um, ah, rather think your mission has been too successful, Vicar,' said the Professor. 'It is so much easier for them to attend your Travelling Church than to travel into Great Pagwell to the main church.'

'Ah,' said the Vicar, 'then perhaps having attracted them to the Travelling Church, we should then bring them here for the service instead of having it in the Travelling Church.'

But that didn't work because the Travelling Church couldn't cope with the rush of people. At each place it visited it was soon filled with people attending the service, but they then got out and the church went on and filled up at the next stop. But when the Vicar started bringing the people to his main church he could, of course, bring only one Travelling Churchful at a time and, by the time he went back and collected another congregation from the next place, the first lot had grown tired of waiting and had gone home.

'We must have a fleet of Travelling Churches!' cried Professor Branestawm.

'Good gracious!' gasped the Vicar. He didn't know whether to be elated, or appalled, or astonished, or doubtful, or mystified at the idea of a fleet of Travelling Churches.

'I don't know what the Bishop will say,' he said.

But the Bishop was too busy arguing with the Dean about the Cathedral roof to say anything.

After several weeks of church-building noises in the Professor's inventory, with Mrs Flittersnoop not knowing what things were coming to, she was sure, but hoped it was all for the best, the fleet of Travelling Churches was ready.

'But I can't drive them all myself,' said the Vicar. 'We must call for volunteers.'

That was easy. Colonel Dedshott instantly offered to drive one, and Commander Hardaport (Retired) reckoned he could navigate a church. Miss Frenzie shot off enthusiastically in one with all bells clanging, and the Mayor found driving a nice quiet restful church rather easier than laying foundation stones and opening bazaars.

So the following Sunday the Vicar had his church full and three-quarters, with people standing and even some lined up outside listening through the windows.

But after a bit the Travelling Churches became redundant because people thought while they were queuing up waiting for them to arrive they might as well queue up for their local bus, which ran rather more frequently, and which stopped right outside Great Pagwell Church.

But the Vicar was delighted. He had a nice full church to preach to, nice fat collections came in, and everybody was happy.

So he gave the Travelling Churches to Pagwell Council, who used them to give old-age pensioners holidays in the country. And the pensioners found the countryside always looked nice and bright and colourful through the stained glass windows whether the sun was shining or not.

Other books by Norman Hunter published in Puffins

THE INCREDIBLE ADVENTURES OF PROFESSOR BRANESTAWM

THE PECULIAR TRIUMPHS OF PROFESSOR BRANESTAWM

PROFESSOR BRANESTAWM ROUND THE BEND

PROFESSOR BRANESTAWM UP THE POLE

PROFESSOR BRANESTAWM'S GREAT REVOLUTION

PROFESSOR BRANESTAWM'S TREASURE HUNT

PROFESSOR BRANESTAWM'S DICTIONARY

THE DRIBBLESOME TEAPOTS

DUST-UP AT THE ROYAL DISCO

THE FRANTIC PHANTOM

PROFESSOR BRANESTAWM'S DO-IT-YOURSELF HANDBOOK

THE PUFFIN BOOK OF MAGIC

PROFESSOR BRANESTAWM'S POCKET MOTOR CAR (Young Puffin)

Some other Puffins you might enjoy

SUPER GRAN, SUPERSTAR

Forrest Wilson

She's on the warpath again: the super senior citizen with X-ray eyes and unbelievable strength! And it's her most difficult assignment yet because the devilish Inventor has got his hands on an invincible shield. Nothing can penetrate it: knives, bullets or death-rays! Only Super Gran can stop the Inventor from conquering the world. But will even her powers be strong enough?

THE BUNCH FROM BANANAS

David Pownall

The steamy coastal town of Santa Margarita del Banana is notable for two things: its bananas, which are world-famous because they curve the other way, and for Bernard the Boy Detective. Bernard's career starts with his brilliant and ingenious ambush of Diablo Dick, who is admittedly the most unsuccessful bandit in history. He solves the most baffling cases, including the theft of Sir George Mindbright Wilderness's entire house, and even manages to foil the High-tailed Red Banana-bending Crows. In fact, the people in Santa Margarita del Banana are a pretty weird bunch.

BAGTHORPES v. THE WORLD

Helen Cresswell

As usual, life is frantic and funny in the zany Bagthorpe household, but great gloom descends when a bank statement arrives indicating an overdraft of millions. With a fervour born of necessity, Mr Bagthorpe plunges his family into a campaign of self-sufficiency, and soon the garden is full of herbs, vegetables and chickens. But it soon becomes clear that all is not well in the garden – Mrs Bagthorpe identifies Tess's lettuces as pansies and snapdragons, while her own flowerbeds bear signs of sprouting beetroot and carrots. Obviously, demon Daisy has been 'helping' again and her good intentions have badly misfired!

MICE AND MENDELSON

Joan Aiken

Mr Mendelson, the Orkney pony, liked thinking about tunes. He specially liked the concerts his two fieldmice friends, Bertha and Gertrude, gave every night on his old piano. But dastardly Dan Sligo had some very unmusical plans for Mr Mendelson's piano, and the two quick-witted mice had to act fast to foil the plot.

I'M TRYING TO TELL YOU

Bernard Ashley

If you had a chance to talk about your school, what would you say . . . honestly? Nerissa, Ray, Lyn and Prakash are all in the same class at Saffin Street School but each of them has something different to say and a different story to tell – all with a real sense of humour that will particularly appeal to readers of about 10.

FANNY AND THE MONSTERS

Penelope Lively

Filled with a burning ambition to be a palaentologist, Fanny had wickedly slipped away from Aunt Caroline's tour of the Crystal Palace to follow an enticing notice, which read: TO THE PREHISTORIC MONSTERS – not pausing to think about the trouble there would be when her disappearance was noticed . . .

Fanny was always getting into trouble of one sort or another. Being the eldest of a large family was bad enough, but being a girl was worse! There were so many exciting and fascinating things to do, none of which were thought suitable for a young lady in Victorian England. Life, thought Fanny, was very unfair.

CODES FOR KIDS

Burton Albert Jr.

A fascinating range of codes and ciphers, all easily coded and yet nearly impossible to break: here is the ideal way to keep prying eyes from your secrets. It is an indispensable handbook for secret agents, generals on the battlefield, high-powered executives, clubs, friends, and anybody with a taste for skulduggery and intrigue.

UP WITH SKOOL!

Who says school's a bad joke? Crammed with jokes, puns and limericks sent in by children from all over the country, *Up With Skool!* shows you the funny side of the place you either love or hate. And ten star personalities contribute their own funny stories of school: read Cyril Smith MP on the delights of school dinners, Harry Secombe on taking up cricket because they needed a sightscreen, Roald Dahl on the amazing punishments handed out at his school, and Roger McGough on the great gollops of information which passed through his head like steam through a football net.

Heard about the Puffin Club?

. . . it's a way of finding out more about Puffin books and authors, of winning prizes (in competitions), sharing jokes, a secret code, and perhaps seeing your name in print! When you join you get a copy of our magazine, *Puffin Post*, sent to you four times a year, a badge and a membership book.
For details of subscription and an application form; send a stamped addressed envelope to:

The Puffin Club Dept A
Penguin Books Limited
Bath Road
Harmondsworth
Middlesex UB7 ODA

and if you live in Australia, please write to:

The Australian Puffin Club
Penguin Books Australia Limited
P.O. Box 257
Ringwood
Victoria 3134